What Others Are Saying

"When Janice first told me what her book was about, my first thought was, 'Well, okay — but what else is there to say about websites? Plus, I just outsource all this stuff.'

"Of course, what I'd conveniently forgotten was what it's like when you first start a business and you're strapped for cash. The ideal is that you'll get an expert to do it for you; the reality is usually somewhat different, unless you're very lucky.

"When I started reading *Cracking The Website Code*, I only got a few pages in and my first thought was, 'I wish this book had been around when I started my business.' Because although there are tons of nerdy, technical manuals about how to code and how to do this, that, and the other, there isn't much at all out there for the 'normal' business owner who needs to know the basics about websites.

"And even if you do get someone else to build your website, you still need to know the basics — otherwise, how do you know what you're getting? How do you know you're not being taken for a ride or sold a lemon?

"Janice's book is filled with smart, practical, simple stuff you need to know about the online world. And the regular exercises mean you actually get stuff done. Unlike so many business books, Janice's focus is on practical actions that make a difference right now.

"If you're a business owner just starting out, and you don't have the budget for a professional web developer, you need to read this book. And if you *do* have the budget, you still need to read this book because you'll be able to stay in full control of your new website as the experts develop it for you."

~ Vicky Fraser, vickyfraser.com, U.K.

"Janice has a way of covering quite a complex topic in a straight forward, sometimes humorous, no nonsense and no hype manner that takes you through a logical and step by step thought process to go through when setting up your website.

"As a marketer, I especially enjoyed the section on the '*10 Essential Ingredients Every Website Needs*' – I wished I had this when I was setting up my website – it's pure gold dust as Janice explains exactly how to make your website pop out to the exact people who are looking for you and what you have to offer. I used to think that my target audience was 'everyone' but Janice teaches you through helpful worksheets how easy and important it is to hone in on your ideal customer or client and how to make them actually *want to buy from you* without them feeling they are being 'sold' to! This one section on its own is worth much more than the cost of the book!!

"I would absolutely recommend this book to anyone who is thinking of revamping their website or starting a website as Janice not only covers the step by step process, but also the essential marketing mindset behind everything she teaches. An essential read for anyone using a website to promote their business!"

~ Nicky Price, diamondmlmtraining.com, U.K.

"I didn't know where to start with setting up a website, I was concerned that I didn't have the knowledge to start and the whole idea worried me. From reading your book I learnt that it wasn't as complicated as I imagined but it did require thought and planning. The book taught me how to plan my content and who to aim it at.

"I liked *The 10 Essential Ingredients Every Website Needs*, my ideas really started to flow by reading that chapter. It made me put pen to paper and I could see that I *could* set up my own website and it wasn't as scary as I thought.

"I also loved the way the book has bullet points and is methodical. Just by reading it you can create and envision how your website is going to look and who your target audience will be and also how to keep people coming back to your website.

"I would definitely recommend the book it really is all you need to set up your website, it's simple to understand and it gives you all the tools you need. There is so much information, it's literally a step by step guide to setting up your own website.

"I loved the way the book was presented; it's very simple to understand, the little quotes from entrepreneurs are great and you finish the book believing not only that you *can* set up a website yourself but that it will be amazing too."

~Louise Paterson, macrosandmuscle.com, U.K.

"For anyone who hasn't yet ventured into the online world (and also for some who have but need some assistance), this book covers all the essential bases, gives practical steps to get started and keep improving, and then leaves the reader with enough information to enable them to delve deeper into the subject (as needed) later on down the track once they're up and running. I highly recommend it.

"I was very impressed with what you've put together. It's a lot of information that is practical and doesn't bog the reader down or turn it into a technical tome. Perfect in other words. If people want the 'super tech' they can go down that rabbit hole on their own.

"I also used the book to turn my mind to a website I've recently created and I'll be running my eye over it again in the weeks to come."

~Aaron Parker, amazingdiscountsdaily.com, Australia

"This book cracks the website and details exactly what you need to do to make any business website a success. If only I had been given this book 8 years ago when I first started building websites for clients - this will shave months if not years off of your online business learning curve.

"What most people who hire a website designer don't understand is that many of the people you can hire out there just 'put a site together' with no consideration to the impact on your business, let alone delivering a focused effort to get your business results.

"*Cracking the Website Code* goes past the technical and mundane, way past, and delivers precise wisdom that can only be gained from years of consulting experience. Whatever Janice is charging for her services she needs to triple them today!"

~ Steve Dimmick, freelancingevolution.com, U.S.A.

"It's very well written. It's not just informative, you also explain very vividly why and how to approach everything. And I really like your writing style!!! You are funny, serious, authentic, convincing and that's great. I'm going to learn a lot from you and your book!"

~Cori Graubaum, graytreemusic.net, Germany

"We didn't even know how to start a website! Teaching us the ins and outs of blogs and optimization, understanding how to look at the analytics and the structure and layout of the site was priceless. We learned how to use the numbers to help grow our market. We also learned we cannot do this on our own and it was a great decision to have a professional like you do it for us. Making us the YouTube videos on how to use WordPress and how to write and optimize the blogs was the very best and I still refer to them.

"You were willing to be very available and patient with us. You made all efforts to listen to our questions and understand them. Even if they were rudimentary for you, you always treated us with respect. You go above and beyond our expectations anytime the call of duty arises. Also, you send us tips and give us tools that to continue to help us, instead of trying to get us to hire you!

"I think that the biggest problem is that people try and do it all themselves. We didn't event know how to find a platform for a website let alone know how to format it."

~Lesley Fahey, seedsupplements.com, U.S.A.

CRACKING The Website CODE

GROW YOUR ONLINE BUSINESS FASTER
WITH A SMARTER WEBSITE AND SAVVY MARKETING

—By—

**JANICE
CUMBERLIDGE**

CRACKING THE WEBSITE CODE

Published by Cracking Publishing
Copyright © Janice Cumberlidge

janice@crackingthewebsitecode.com
www.crackingthewebsitecode.com

Cover illustration © 2016 Kath Walker Illustration.

Cracking The Website Code / Janice Cumberlidge — 1st edition.
ISBN 978-0-9954524-0-4

Dedication

This book is dedicated to my husband, Steve, and to my mum and dad, for allowing me to indulge myself in my writing for weeks on end, all the time staying fully supportive of my end goal.
Thank you.

I also dedicate this to a man who influenced me throughout my teenage years, right up to the present day —a man who may have been small in stature but will always be huge in my heart—Prince.
R.I.P.

Acknowledgements

I'd like to say a big thank you to my very talented
friend, Kath Walker, who created the wonderful
illustration of me sat on top of the world,
laptop in hand, for the front cover.
Thanks for the tiny waist too!
Brilliant work, highly recommended.
Visit her at kathwalker-illustration.co.uk

Also, thanks to my lovely proof-readers for spotting
my little typos and letting me know if I was getting my
points across well enough. Apparently I was, so blame
them if you don't agree. They each deserve a drink of their
choice, which I will put my hand in my pocket for, if and
when we meet up next.

Contents

Your Free Gift

Thank You For Purchasing
Cracking The Website Code

To help guide you on your quest to improve your website and grow your online business, I've created a **free companion workbook** and **set of downloads** to accompany this book, which can be accessed instantly at the link below.

Inside the workbook, you will find the exercises that relate to the chapters in the book, making it easy to find the section you need as you read along.

These free gifts will enable you to speed your path to getting better results from your website, so I encourage you to take advantage of them by downloading them before you start reading.

**For free access to the
companion workbook and downloads, visit:**

http://crackingthewebsitecode.com/bonus

Preface

A website for your business—you know you need one and in fact these days it's almost criminal not to have one. If you want yours to have the ability to sky-rocket your business, you need to know what you're doing with it and more importantly, why.

In this book I will be laying out the essentials every entrepreneur needs to know about how to design a website that draws in visitors and converts them into sales or subscribers, all while you sleep. I'll present ideas in a conversational and non-technical manner, which should mean it's an easy read for you.

By the time you've finished this book, my intention and ultimate wish is that you have clarity on exactly what you need to put into place so that you can go on to make a website that works harder for you, bringing you the success you so desire.

Creating a website is only the *start* of the process of growing any online business, and it's important to see the bigger picture of what it takes to succeed. By picking up this book, you're indicating that you *do* want a prosperous future for your business, and that's not only admirable, it's essential if your business is to survive in this crazy digital world.

After absorbing the content of this book, your next move *must* be to act on what you've learned. Knowledge is in fact *not* power, unless you apply that learning. By taking positive steps to put the theories I present into practice, you will have a much greater chance of bringing in more business through your website. Of course, as with anything in life, nothing is guaranteed, but those who put the effort in are much more likely to get to where they want to be than those taking zero action.

I've been a software engineer for over 22 years and a web designer and developer for over 14, so I can almost do this with my eyes closed. But I know from experience of guiding others that web design may not come naturally, in fact it can be a scary prospect. If it's not the fear of the unknown that puts the willies up you, it may be the overwhelm of having so much else to do in your business that you just can't seem to make progress. Trust me, you're not alone in either of these.

This book takes you from getting online if you don't

already have a web presence, through identifying who your website is truly aimed at, and on to creating a site that brings those exact people to you in their droves, ready to devour your carefully designed content. I've included chapters on the peripheral activities that can't be ignored when talking about website design, including marketing, selling and keeping the bogeyman at bay. Okay, maybe not the bogeyman, but unscrupulous hackers at least.

If you're totally new to website creation, I believe it's a skill you can pick up if it's presented in the right way. But you will need solid determination and the will to succeed, because it can't half test your patience at times.

If, after reading this book, you decide that creating your own website is not something you want to pursue, you will still have a valuable insight you can use, to instruct a web designer on what to create on your behalf. Armed with this knowledge, you'll be able to talk with a confidence and level of understanding that most business owners will never achieve, which will get you the service you deserve and also prevent you from getting ripped off.

If implemented strategically, creating a great website *will* help you grow your business, which could have you well on your way to gaining more customers, a greater income and the life you maybe currently only dream of.

The best way I can help you with your website is by showing you how to help yourself. But you will only get the results if you put in the work. So please follow up your good intentions with some focused action.

Writing this book has been almost therapeutic. For so long I've wanted to share my knowledge but until now have kept it locked up in my brain, only accessible by myself and my clients. Now I get to share my insights with you and help way more people than I ever could by taking on client websites single-handedly. It's win-win.

I hope you enjoy reading this book as much as I have loved writing it.

Introduction

Why do you want to learn how to create your perfect website? What results are you missing in your business, that having a fully-functional, well-designed marketing machine could help bring? And what is it that's *really* stopping you seeing results?

Most business owners want the same thing—more customers, more sales and more eyes on their product or service. I want that too, which is honestly one of the reasons I'm writing this book. In presenting my knowledge of all things web-related, I will be empowering business owners like you to take the life of your website into your own hands. And for me that's another reason for writing this book—I know the power a website can bring and I *love* seeing people succeed with theirs.

Almost everyone has a website these days and many do fantastically with theirs, so why not you? It can be one of the best ways to boost your business but admittedly also one of the most frustrating to get right. A common problem is lack of knowledge on how to go about creating a site that is in tune with your customers' needs — one that delivers both what *they* want and what *you* need to grow your business. A web presence alone is simply not enough—your website should be thought of as just one element of a complete marketing system, and you can't possibly appreciate what's involved in completing the full picture without some education and experience. That's what I aim to fast track you towards.

A Bit of Background

When I started fiddling with computers in a useful way —as opposed to playing Dickie's Diamonds on the Commodore 64 when I was a teenager—it was for my first real, grown-up job. I had graduated from Loughborough University with a degree in Mathematical Engineering and walked straight into a job in a computing department at a large engineering firm. This was around 1993 and back then, computers were more akin to having a tumble dryer sat on your desk. The noise of the whirring machine with its ginormous monitor and clunky keyboard were not only like something left over from the eighties, they actually *were* left over from the eighties. And so were many of the staff. It was your typical geeky software job and I was one of just two girls in what was predominantly a man's world.

I have to admit I didn't think I'd enjoy computing to start with, but with a logical mind that likes to work out puzzles and tick off lists, this acted in my favour and I quickly learned how to write organised blocks of code.

Around 14 years ago I started designing websites for individuals and for small businesses, coding everything by hand and designing every last little element from scratch, because I could. I resisted the lure of the spanking new plug-and-play framework of WordPress for as long as possible—in my mind I was a programmer and I was darn good at it and I didn't want to give in to the black-box approach that WordPress offered. But in the end curiosity finally got the better of me and after a few tentative trials came the a-ha moment—I saw the light and became a convert.

WordPress not only enabled me to develop websites much quicker, but the increasing number of pre-designed templates available meant that I could get a head start on a design and give clients a very early preview of their finished site. I can now honestly say I'll never go back to the coding days of old, I'm 100% WordPress to my core. Cut me open and you'll see.

My problem is that I'm only one person and can only take on so much work, which is one of the main reasons I decided to put together this book—so that people like you, who are keen to learn, can pick up a stack of savvy information you can apply to your website, to improve your understanding and bolster your skill set.

Anyone can make an attempt at creating a website, but I want to help you do it *really* well, so that you can cut out some of the trial and error, and avoid making the same mistakes as many others who have gone before you.

Who This Book Is For

This book was written with a definite reader in mind. Hopefully you see yourself in one of the following categories:

- You're an entrepreneur who is feeling uneasy at the prospect of putting together a new website.
- You've started a website but are seeing limited results and want to figure out what to change to boost your chances of success.
- You want the knowledge and confidence to turn your site into something to be proud of, that your visitors will love.
- You're trying to decide if designing your own website is right for you.
- You want to learn strategies that will bring in more leads, clients and sales to your website.

If any of the above points ring true with you, you're in the right place.

Of course there are also people who won't be suited to reading this book, and that's ok—it's not *for* everyone. Let me briefly outline who may *not* benefit.

Who This Book Is NOT For

- Anyone afraid of hard work. Putting together a website takes time, some deep thought, business analysis, decision making and a little bit of money, so if you're not prepared for any of these, now's the time to close the cover.
- Anyone expecting a set of step-by-step instructions on setting up a WordPress website. Although I give you many strategies on how to run your website more effectively, this book is not intended as an instructional or installation guide.
- Anyone wanting to weigh up the pros and cons of all the various website platforms. All tips I provide are specifically based on the WordPress framework, as this is my area of expertise.
- Competent WordPress web designers who already know it all. Having said that, this book is not just about website design in the traditional sense but also goes much deeper into the whys and hows of marketing and customer psychology. So if you're a web designer with limited marketing background, you may still get some value.

You're still reading, so let's have a look at how you can get the most out of the ensuing chapters.

How To Use This Book

If you want to create a fabulous, fully functional website that works for your business, I recommend you read this book cover to cover and do the actionable exercises as you read. These are also available to print out and fill in at the bonus link given at the back of the book. You may dip in and out of any section at any time but it will all make more sense when taken in the order presented.

In Chapter 1 we'll take a look at what owning a website is really all about and the many ways it can truly benefit your business.

Chapters 2-4 will take you from deciding if creating a website yourself is right for you, through choosing the perfect domain name and getting online with WordPress.

Once you've got your website up and running, you will benefit hugely from chapters 5-7, where we'll look at the essential ingredients for any website, how to tap into what your ideal client is looking for when they visit and how to make it look great and function well.

Then comes the part that many entrepreneurs don't get round to—marketing your website. Chapters 7-11 show you how to get your content seen and how to write in a way that makes your audience fall in love with you and want to buy from you. We'll also look at *the* most important way to secure your business for the future.

With a brief look at website safety and security, we'll end in Chapter 13 with six opportunities to make more money from your website, some of which can be implemented in under 5 minutes.

Although I refer to costs throughout the book in British pounds, I realise that you may be more familiar with U.S. dollar amounts, so I have included those in brackets too, using an exchange rate that was reasonably accurate at the time of writing. These will look something like this: £10 ($15). Exchange rates and costs are subject to change, so please check before making any purchases.

At the back of the book you will find links to the resources I refer to in some of the chapters, including the free companion workbook and the list of essential WordPress plugins. I recommend you download these now so you can refer to them as you read along.

Once again, the only way you will get real value and improved results from reading this book is if you take action to implement what you learn.

Let's get cracking the website code.

Definitions

Internet
ˈɪntənɛt/
noun

a global computer network providing a variety of information and communication facilities, consisting of interconnected networks using standardised communication protocols.

World Wide Web
noun

an information system on the Internet which allows documents to be connected to other documents by hypertext links, enabling the user to search for information by moving from one document to another.

website
ˈwɛbsʌɪt/
noun

a location connected to the Internet that maintains one or more web pages.

Why Have A Website Anyway?

"A bad web site is like a grumpy salesperson"
~ Jakob Nielsen

Why do you want a website? And, more importantly, why do you want a *good* website?

Visibility. Credibility. Sales potential.

Those are just 3 reasons.

But before those benefits come to fruition, there is often a steep learning curve that many people just don't anticipate.

After starting a website and running into some

inevitable issues, the most common emotion that ensues is confusion, frequently followed by frustration. This often stems from lack of knowledge or understanding, or both. Creating a website is definitely a worthwhile activity but if it doesn't go as you'd hoped, the process can leave you deflated and even feeling like a failure.

With a bit of help and nurturing, entrepreneurs just like you can be lifted from the depths of website hell into the realms of success you'd previously imagined. So let's first look some of the reasons for getting online that you simply can't ignore, starting with why the internet holds the key to your future.

Could You Be One In A Billion?

Let's make the distinction between the Internet, the World Wide Web (the Web or WWW) and a website, as they're all related but subtly different.

The Internet is a worldwide network of millions of computers—the enabler for communications, and the Web is the mechanism that allows us to hop from one part of the Internet to another. The term 'website' refers to a collection of files stored somewhere on the Internet.

The Internet dates back to 1958, when the United States government set up their Advanced Research Projects Agency (ARPA) to explore science and technology ideas. Communication trials started between just two computers and it wasn't until 1991 that the Web was publicly announced.

Things didn't catch on very quickly and it was estimated that two years later, there were just 623 websites. But incredibly, even after thirteen years, over a billion Internet users had got online, and by September 2014 over a billion unique websites existed. That number can really blow your mind.

No one actually owns the Internet outright, so this global phenomenon of an interconnected series of networks really is a feat of engineering and technology, and a great example of the world working as one. It's a shame we don't work as well together on world peace, but that's an issue for a completely different book!

As you can see from the above statistics, the competition is intense and it's now more important than ever to make sure your website stands out and gets seen amongst the plethora of others.

Let's take a look at what benefits having a website can bring and why you should have one at all.

Online Sales Brochure

When you go to buy a book, how do you decide if it's the right one for you? You probably start by looking at the cover, title and subtitle, and quickly making a first impression. You decide within seconds whether it appeals. If the front cover looks good and the title grabs you, you'll probably read the blurb on the back to get more information. If the author is able to grab your attention by turning on an emotion deep inside or by identifying with one or more of your areas of interest, you're highly likely to open or even buy the book so you can read more.

The same process of discovery happens when someone visits your website. Your visitor quickly makes a first decision based on what's immediately visible on the page they land on. If this has a positive feel, they may scroll down to read more, until eventually they delve deeper into your site by clicking links and reading more of the innermost pages. If they get this far, you have effectively sold your site to them, based on your successful presentation. You've shown your visitor your online sales brochure and it held their interest.

Your website is where you get to showcase your products or services and present them in the exact way *you* decide. No one can come and mess up your window display and it should be set up to feature the best you have to offer, in the most attractive way. Your storefront is completely under your control—or at least it should be— make sure this is the case.

Put your best offerings in the most prominent places. Be concise yet informative. Draw the reader in deeper in a careful and considered manner. Give them an experience they're likely to value and remember.

Once you master the art of thinking from a visitor's point of view and tailoring your site to flow in the best possible way, that's when it truly becomes your online sales brochure, effectively selling itself. That's also when your hard work and understanding will start bringing you more leads, customers and return visitors.

24x7 Sales Machine

One thing that a successful website owner will know is how good it feels to wake up to new sales notification emails. Making sales while you sleep is an unbelievable motivator to getting your website done. Once the first sale trickles in, then another and another, you'll be addicted to the feeling and will never want it to stop.

But having a 24x7 sales machine is not as simple as just putting some products on a webpage and waiting for the buyers to arrive. It takes much more work and it's often the effectiveness of your marketing that brings in many of those sales, rather than the website alone.

Think of your website as the enabler to those sales, the place where it all happens. Set your site up with attractive and pertinent content, with a good flow. Treat it as your sales brochure and you will be set to maximise the potential of anyone who does visit. Then think of the work you do in getting correctly targeted traffic to your site and the follow-up activities as the mechanism by which the sale is enabled.

Whether you use email marketing, traffic from social media or paid advertisements, one thing is for certain— you don't often get sales by accident. This is why having a successful website is not solely about getting the technical and visual aspects correct, and is also why, in this book, I've included chapters about the broader picture of marketing your website. Only once you put all the pieces of the jigsaw together will you see things start to fall into place and your hard work really pay off.

Status Symbol

Some things never go out of fashion—Champagne seems to be one of them. The who's-who can often be seen sipping on a glass of expensive golden bubbles—and that's the point—they make sure they're *seen* with only the best. It's a status symbol they love to associate with, no matter how bitter it tastes or how much it may cost.

Can you imagine how horrified these same people would feel if they were ever caught on camera pouring from a bottle of cheap Cava? But the truth is that in a blind taste test, Cava has been proven to win time and time again, so the point is that the contents of the bottle may actually be terrific, but it's the *perceived* quality that people get hung up on. They want to associate with something of status, something that rightly or wrongly elevates their own imagined value in the world.

On your website, whether you like it or not, people make their first judgements based on perceived quality, so if your website looks cheap or flung together without much consideration, you're likely to be thought of as being at the bargain basement end of the market. As you can imagine, this only appeals to a certain clientele—and this *may* not be the type you intend to attract. But turn your website into something to be proud to be associated with and you're more likely to gain higher quality paying clients from it. That's not to say clients who pay more are any easier to work with, they're often not!

If you have a website already, have a look at it with fresh eyes. Does it speak quality or does it give off an air of *anything goes*? It might be time for a rethink if it's the latter.

Communicate Your Brand Values

Whether your site is selling products, services or simply serving as an information centre, it's one of your prime methods of communicating with your customers.

If you write a blog, this is a great way to communicate, as you can deliver new information to your loyal fans, which fosters trust in you over a period of time. Visitors who decide that you have enough to offer may sign up for your mailing list, which enables you to follow up with further communications and sales pitches later.

Communication is not always written or verbal, but can be instilled into images, styles and other visual triggers. By keeping your branding consistent across your website and all other channels, your customers will quickly get to recognise your content at a glance and feel an affinity towards you. Your brand will feel like a familiar friend and this is what will keep them coming back for more.

You only have to look at some of the images Starbucks puts out on their Instagram account and you'll see examples of what I mean—attractive coffee products shown in the familiar, consistently styled surroundings of one of their comfortable shops, with the Starbucks logo on prime display. You know exactly what to expect when you visit their Instagram, their website and their coffee shops alike, and that's why you can switch between all locations seamlessly.

Think of your website and brand as an extension of your audible voice. It's great to get your message across in many different ways, just be sure you communicate consistently and often, so your visitors get to know you.

EXERCISE 1.1:
Assess Your Branding

Take a look at your branding across all the different platforms on which you have a presence. This may include social media channels, your website, printed materials, digital downloads and so on. Ask yourself:

- Does the look and feel of your website match those of your social media profile(s)?
- Are you being consistent with the colours and typefaces you use?
- Can a visitor to your website instantly recognise your content's style, based on what you've shared elsewhere?

If you identify any inconsistencies between your online profiles, make sure to fix those straight away. If you do this, your followers and website visitors will appreciate

and understand what you stand for much more easily, bringing greater trust and helping you to become the consistent and familiar brand you are aiming for.

Credibility

If you're an expert in your field, or want to become known as one, your website is a perfect place to position yourself as such. What better arena than your own corner of the internet to stamp your authority on your niche.

Organic traffic to your site—organic meaning naturally occurring rather than traffic you paid for—often comes from searches via Google, and you can bet that a good proportion of those searches are made by people looking to find information. So if your site can provide a full and meaningful answer to their question, that makes you the expert in their eyes. You knew something that they didn't and now they more than likely respect you for sharing that knowledge.

A website can also provide credibility for you as an authority in your field. If, for example, you're an individual who designs wedding invitations, you may have been doing this in your spare time and getting work by recommendation, but as soon as you put your wedding invitation design services on a website—boom!—you have instant credibility as both a *real* business and also as an expert in your field.

Don't underestimate the value a website can bring and how it can launch you as a go-to authority. And when it does, it's probably time to start charging more—you're the expert and you earned that title, so don't be shy.

You Can't Afford NOT To

I'm throwing this one in just in case you're reading this and wondering if having a website is right for you at all.

Think back. If you were wondering whether to take the plunge ten or fifteen years ago, you may have had a tough decision—it may not have actually mattered if you had a site or not. If you were a coffee shop owner or a butcher, you probably didn't need a website as most people just called in to your business when they wanted to. And if they needed to know your opening times there was always the Yellow Pages.

But with the dramatic rise in use of mobile phones and tablet computers, cyberspace is where people now look first for your opening times or what you have to offer. And with almost every other business in your niche probably already having a website, the last thing you want to do is get left behind. By not having a site you'd be hiding the light of what you have to offer under a rather large internet-shaped bushel. And who would know where to look for you then, especially as the Yellow Pages is now nothing more than an unwanted lump in the recycling bin?

So if you're not sure whether you need a website or not, I would ask you if you're serious about your business. If you answer positively, it's time to invest a little effort into getting a website set up. Without it you'll always be one step behind the competition and one thing is certain— you'll never get any new customers through my friend Mr. Google, as you won't even show up in his big list of possibilities.

What are you waiting for?

Chapter 1: Summary

1. **The Internet is a rapidly expanding marketplace.** If you were ever unsure about the need for a web presence for your business, now's the time to ditch those fears and get online. The Internet waits for no one.

2. **Treat your website as your sales brochure.** When customers arrive on your virtual doorstep, give them something to hang around for. Identify with their problems, show how you can help them and make it appealing. Don't waste your piece of virtual real estate.

3. **Engineer your sales machine.** Sales don't happen by accident and if you want to enjoy sales while you sleep, you need to put effective campaigns in place to get people to your site. Your site then needs to offer what was expected, in order to convert to cold hard cash.

4. **People are snobs.** Your site should be a positive place where people feel like they're mixing with the best. Anything too shabby will turn off visitors and leave you high and dry. Make your site something to be proud of, that your visitors will love.

5. **Communicate well.** Your brand and values must come across effectively to your visitors in order for them to get to know you. Make sure you communicate using multiple methods, often, so that visitors and sales come more readily.

6. **Stamp your authority.** Your website can launch you from small-time amateur to respected professional, so take it seriously and make the most of the web's ability to boost your visibility, expertise and credibility.

7. **Just get a website!** Every type of business can benefit from having a website, you just need to appreciate its potential. Take action today.

Can You Really Make A
Website Yourself?

*"Whether you think that you can, or that
you can't, you are usually right."*
~ Henry Ford

People who believe in themselves and their abilities tend
to achieve way more than those who are down on
themselves from the outset. I don't know what approach
you take towards difficult tasks but as Henry Ford
indicated in his quote above, whether you think you're cut
out for creating your own website or not, you're *usually*

right.

In this chapter we'll look at how to make the decision of whether to go DIY with your website or to have a professional take on the job for you. Firstly, let's look at the question of if you can *really* do this yourself.

Is DIY For You?

Let's see. This is a book for entrepreneurs so I'm guessing you're already an entrepreneur or are at least doing your best to become one. That tells me you have the will to try new things and to create your own path in life. So I'd say yes, you *can* create your own website, if it's something that you *want* to do for yourself.

However, you might be someone who is perfectly capable of setting up your own website, but it might not be best for you to take it on. If you're already used to outsourcing tasks that you know you're *not* ideally suited to, you might spot that designing a website is another such opportunity. This would be a smart move as it frees you up to concentrate on what you're best at, which is probably managing your day-to-day business.

When deciding if creating and managing your website yourself is for you, here are a few points to think about:

- **Do you have the desire or inclination to do it yourself?** If you've never had a good relationship with computers or technology, the initial site creation might not be for you, but weekly content updates may be more manageable.

- **Do you have time to spend on the initial website creation and set up?** This can be anywhere from 2 to 30 or more hours, depending on the complexity of the website and the number of pages you want to create.
- **Can you commit to writing regular content updates and taking care of maintenance activities?** After getting online, this is the crucial part that you can't afford to slack on and it can take anywhere from 4 to 40 hours a month, depending on how much content you wish to create.

With the leaps in technology and the ease with which you can create your own website today, it's more common than ever to go DIY if you have the motivation and desire to do so. Yes, there are quite a few steps involved in setting up a website and getting everything just right, but nothing is beyond your abilities if you come with a positive attitude and willingness to learn.

If you're not yet sure whether you want to create your own website or outsource the work, I suggest you weigh up all that you read in this book and then make the decision once you're armed with all the facts. The time spent creating a website can be both frustrating and fulfilling, but I know it's not for everyone. You just have to figure out which camp you're in and go for it.

If you decide to employ someone to do it for you

instead, you'll want to digest the rest of this chapter to learn what you need to ask potential web designers, what they should ask you, and how much it's likely to set you back.

Outsourcing

From talking to other business owners, I know some of the horrors that can come out of hiring someone to do even a relatively simple website design. If you hire the wrong person, you may end up feeling disappointed, and even worse, you may have to hire someone better qualified to fix it up all over again. This alone is reason enough never to hire family to have a go for you, because having a go is not good enough, unless web design and marketing is what they do in their everyday job.

Many problems can stem from not asking the right questions before hiring someone to create your site for you. Having a designer that you gel with and who understands your business goals is key. Just as important is that they have the right skills to design good looking sites that contain the essential elements of design and copy to bring in the leads and sales you need. This means having solid marketing skills as well as the obvious technical abilities.

There is one problem with hiring any web designer - they probably won't have anywhere near as much invested in the outcome of their work as you do. Put simply, no one cares about your business as much as you, and that's why it's important to find someone you trust, should you decide to outsource.

Aren't Web Designers Expensive? (And An Aside About Money)

There are some excellent web designers out there who don't charge enough. I'll hold my hand up and say I was one of them for a long time. It's not that I didn't think my work was good enough, I was just really uncomfortable asking for money. I guess I didn't like the possibility that someone might say no and they'd tell me it was because I was too expensive, so I took the easy option and kept my fees low. Needless to say, as the word spread, I was forever being asked to take on new website designs because my designs were top quality but my prices were crazily low. And although being in demand feels great, it isn't fulfilling to allow yourself to be taken advantage of and it certainly doesn't pay the bills.

Running a business means that you have to get past any money blocks if you ever hope to make a living from it. You have to accept that you might get knock backs and this also means not getting upset by them. If you don't win every contract, so what? It probably doesn't mean the quality of your work isn't good enough, it just means that you didn't sell yourself well enough on that occasion. Marketing is not just selling *things*, you have to be able to sell yourself too.

That was a little off track but I thought worth sharing,

in case you feel you're in a similar situation in your business right now. Charge what you're worth, it's your duty to yourself.

Taking that into account, the decision of which web designer to employ clearly cannot be simply based on price. I will say that you *usually* get what you pay for, but after telling you my story above, you'll see there are occasions when that's not always true. The best way to decide if a web designer is the one for you is to ask lots of questions, so let's take a look at what those might be.

What To Ask A Web Designer

To help you employ the right designer for you, here are the questions you should ask potential suitors:

- **Can I see examples of your previous work?** Check these websites out and make sure the person did actually create them. You can even take the time to contact a couple of the website owners to ask if they would recommend using this person or company.
- **When can you start work on my website?** If the designer is booked up in advance, it can be a good sign that they're in demand, but you don't want to wait forever.
- **What timescale can you finish my site in?** This will often depend on how cooperative you can be in assisting with things that come up along the way, but as a rough guide, I usually quote an average of

4-8 weeks for most sites, or 2-4 months for sites with more complexity or greater number of pages. This allows a couple of weeks for gathering all the requirements, deciding on the look & feel and planning out the layout, content and functionality. The remaining time is then used to work on creating the site and collaborating with the business owner to firm up the final solution. At the end, I allow a week for the business owner to test the site and come back with anything that they would like changing before we officially launch it. Obviously, all web designers will work to their own timescales and with their own methodology but as long as you are aware of their process and understand the extent of the involvement you will both have at each stage, the details can be worked out between you.

- **What access will I have to my website after it's completed?** You need to decide if you want the designer to hand over the full control of the site to you, or if you still want them to look after the maintenance of it afterwards. There are different levels of access they could give you, the highest being an Administrator and a lower level being an Author. I rarely give my clients admin access to the website if they want to keep me on to maintain it, as admin means access-all-areas, and that can spell trouble if you don't know what you're doing. I prefer to give enough access so the business owner can create new blog posts, add new products to their store and other basic everyday tasks. I keep the site design and maintenance in my own safe hands.

- **What experience in marketing do you have?** If they say they're just a web designer and if you're also not experienced in writing good copy, you might want to look for someone else. I can't stress highly enough how important the marketing side of website design is—if you don't get this part right, your website could be a major flop no matter how pretty it looks.

- **What is the cost of the site design and implementation and are there any ongoing fees?** After talking through your requirements and goals with the web designer, it's quite normal for them to give you a proposal document, where they detail all the items you've talked about and agreed, as well as the costs. Check that the quote is broken down into initial site design and implementation costs, plus any extra fees such as website hosting or annual maintenance. Also check the hourly or monthly rates for any additional work such as adding new functionality or changing the design. Make sure you're happy you understand all costings before you sign on the dotted line.

You must feel comfortable with your chosen web designer as you will be having regular conversations with them. Designing a site is not just a matter of gathering requirements then handing over the finished product, it takes collaboration so good communication is a must.

Lastly, before you hire someone based on all the above, there are a few things that it's important your web designer asks you. And if they don't... run for the hills. Let's take a look at what they are.

What A Web Designer Should Ask You

Any decent web designer will want to find out as many details about your website project and your business as possible. Ideally, they will start from a similar place you did when you were defining your business and goals, and that is finding out about who your clients are, what makes them tick, why they will visit your website and what the goals and desired outcomes are.

In short, if your web designer is to give you the quality of site you hope they will, they'll need lots of information from you. If they don't ask for any, it's most definitely not a good indicator for the future.

Here are some of the questions you should be asked by anyone who has your best interests at heart:

- **Who are your ideal clients?**
- **What does your website aim to solve for your visitors?**

- What are your visitors coming to your site for?
- What are the short, medium and long term goals of your business and your website?
- Do you, as a business owner, have time to answer questions and review progress on an ongoing basis?
- What timescale do you need me to get the job done in and do you have an absolute deadline?
- What access do you require once the site is complete? i.e. will I be handing you the virtual keys or would you like me to maintain it for you?

If you're happy your designer has gathered information pertaining to all the above questions, if you're confident that the web designer's previous work is of a standard you aspire to, and if the costings suit your budget, you may have found your perfect web designer, congratulations!

How Much Should It Cost?

As there is such a variation in requirements from website to website and a great differential between the services and quality in the marketplace, this is a difficult question to answer.

What I can tell you is that websites are not cheap if done properly and by a reputable designer. As a rough guide I've seen incredibly simple websites made from fixed templates, offered for around £200 ($300). This of course means that nothing is tailored to you and the hope is that this off-the-shelf design is already optimised for your needs and market. It probably won't be the type of site you would design if you had a larger budget, but for some, this approach can get them started.

For a bespoke website, you can expect to pay anything from a few hundred to a few thousand pounds, depending on your requirements and who you hire.

The way to make sure you're getting not only the service and website you want but also the best price, is to shop around and get at least three quotes. You can then weigh up what each is offering and what your gut feeling tells you about them. Just don't rush in and take the first quote you get because you think it sounds fair—if you've nothing to compare to, how do you know?

Chapter 2: Summary

- **Decide if creating a website is right for you.** Don't start it if you're impatient or a technophobe, you won't last long!

- **Choose carefully when hiring a designer.** Go armed with your list of questions so that you get the best service at the best price.

- **Be prepared to spend time creating content.** A website doesn't just happen, it needs careful planning and content for each page. Make sure to get together everything you need before getting started, it will save a lot of back and forth later.

- **Know the costs up front.** Be sure to learn exactly what your website will set you back each month, whether you're designing it yourself or having someone do it for you. Maintenance contracts can be expensive so get your deal in writing.

What You Need To Know About Getting Online

"The only way to do great work is to love what you do."
~ Steve Jobs

One of the most exciting moments of getting online is quite possibly the process of choosing your domain name. This is when it all starts to feel more real and you know your shiny, new website is within reach. Once the domain is officially yours, you're just a few clicks away from seeing your name, brand or product live on the internet.

If you're prone to over-analysing, you may actually find the whole idea of choosing a single name for your site quite impossible! But if you follow my tips in this chapter, you'll be able to weed out the no-no names and be sure that the one you end up with will be something you can be proud to be associated with and that will last as your brand grows.

So let's take a look at choosing and registering your domain name, and how you then turn it from just a name into a live website using WordPress.

What's In A (Domain) Name?

A domain name is the part commonly found right after the www. part of a web address. As an example, google is the domain name of the website www.google.com.

As well as considering which domain name you'd like for your website, you'll also need to chose your extension —that's the last part of the name, something like .com or .co.uk. The most popular extension is .com as it signifies a global presence and seems to be the most desirable to own. Each country has their own specific extension, such as .com.au for Australia or .co.uk for the United Kingdom. The extension .com is the one most people will try if they're not sure what your website extension is, so I would always try to get the .com even if you also register your local country extension too.

If you decide to register the same domain name with

more than one extension, you don't need to create several versions of your website. You can simply create your website on the domain you favour the most, then set up your secondary domains with forwarding. This will redirect any traffic that lands on any of your secondary domains to your one main website where all your content lives.

It's worth noting that there are some more unusual extensions that you might like to consider for special purposes or events, such as .christmas or .london. With these being relatively new to the market and not as widely used, you're more likely to find that your desired domain name is free for registration. There are more of these special domains being released every few months so look out for them being announced by domain registration or web hosting companies.

Choosing An Appropriate Name

Your domain name will identify your brand, company, product or service for years to come so it's important to choose wisely. For those who wish to use their personal name or company name as their website domain, the decision may just be as easy as checking if anyone else has already registered that name, and if not, you're in luck and your domain name is an easy pick.

If your website is to represent a product or service, this is when you have more creative licence over the name you choose. But this can also be when it becomes more tricky as there are so many possibilities available to you.

One approach to finding the perfect domain name is to first brainstorm a list of keywords related to your niche. Then you can try combinations of any 2, 3 or 4 of these keywords to come up with some catchy and memorable possibilities. Using keywords that are likely to be typed into the search engines may also help your website be found easier, so this is worth considering when choosing a name.

Here are a few points to note when coming up with a shortlist of potential winners:

- **Shorter domain names are usually better**. Think ahead to when you're announcing your website name to the world—the shorter and more catchy it is, the easier it will roll off the tongue. Try to keep domain names to 2, 3 or at most 4 words.

- **Try not to use hyphens in your domain name**— imagine verbally telling a customer your website address and having to say all those hyphens in between the words—not easy to say is it?

- **Write out the domain name in lowercase letters** and see if there's any ambiguity in the meaning or if it just doesn't look right when the words are mashed together. For example, if you have a store called Jess' Shoes you probably shouldn't go for jessshoes.com. For a start, there are too many "s" characters in the middle and there's also ambiguity when you glance at the name—does she have a penchant for fashionable footwear or is she a keen gardener (Jess's Hoes)? If your domain name is not immediately understood visually, it may put people off visiting your site and they will also not easily be able to direct friends to it.

- **Try not to use numbers within a domain name**. When you tell someone the website name, do they put the number or do they write the number out in words? For example, is it 8ball.com or eightball.com?

- **Try to avoid words that also sound like numbers or letters**—for example for and 4, you and u, eye and i—the less chance for misinterpretation, the better. For example, would an eyewear company choose eyeforglasses, i4glasses or eye4glasses? None of these would be perfect if they wanted to avoid customer confusion.

- **Try to use words with positive ramifications** rather than negative, as people are often swayed by the prospect of benefit or gain rather than disappointment or loss.

- **Say the domain name out loud**. Hear it, imagine it, sense how you would feel saying it to someone who doesn't yet know your business. Does it sound right? Does it feel right in your gut? If not, don't take the chance with it as you may regret it later.

- **Make your domain future proof**. If there's a possibility you may diversify or introduce new products or services into your business in the future, your domain name should be something that is not too specific to your original product— that is, unless you make the business decision to set up a new site for every product, which can sometimes be ideal for launching brand new items to the world when you don't want to cross over with your other products. If you know how your business will grow, try to pick a name that encompasses all that you intend to do. It's best to pick a name that doesn't constrain you later on. For example, you may choose bakedtreats.com rather than bakedcookies.com if you thought you may later want to expand your range and not to have to start a sister website.

Handy Helpers

There are a few novel ways of coming up with domain names and quickly checking their availability, using online tools. The following websites are my favourite handy helpers.

impossibility.org

If you have a keyword you want to use but are flexible on the full domain name, Impossibility can help. Type in a word and it will search for domain availability using your word plus any other noun or adjective, either prepended or appended to it.

As an example, I typed in the keyword "flower" and asked it to give me all available domains with 4 letter adjectives on the end of my word. There were some interesting results but one domain it found was flowerdaft.com, which I thought could be a fun name for a website dedicated to all things flowery.

knowem.com

This is another availability tool but covers a wider set of options. Type in a domain name and Knowem will check all the popular web domain extensions, over 500 social media account usernames and even the trademark database for availability, so you can instantly see if the name you like is available across multiple platforms.

Knowem is free to use but there are paid options, for which Knowem will set up all the accounts for you and even fill in your bio details. This can save you a considerable amount of time if you want more than a handful of associated social media accounts. The done-for-you options are fairly pricey though, so if you're just starting out it's probably best to save your money and spend a little time registering and setting up all the accounts for yourself.

bustaname.com

If you have a list of keywords related to your product or niche, give Bustaname a try. Enter your keywords then let it search for domain availability for every combination of these keywords. You can instruct it to find two or three word combinations and can specify which domain extensions to check.

With BustAName, there are even options to try more unusual names by appending -ly, -ster or -let to your keyword, or to remove the last vowel. This idea of purposely mis-spelling a word or adding an extension to find a unique domain name is currently trending, some examples being infographly.com and foundr.com.

Be aware that if you do consider an unusual spelling or word ending, your audience may not immediately grasp your attempts at originality and you risk losing visitors due to mis-typing in the address bar. That was exactly what happened to photo sharing website, flickr.com, owned by Yahoo. When the company realised it was losing a lot of users to the similarly spelled flicker.com, they took the bold but very expensive decision to acquire the domain flicker.com, which was already registered by someone else. After a lengthy law suit, it's reported to have cost Yahoo around $600,000 to finally get this domain under their control. If you visit flicker.com today, you will be redirected straight to flickr.com, which makes it a very expensive domain forwarder! I bet they wish they'd considered these costly implications before choosing their domain name!

Purchasing Your Domain

Once you've chosen your favourite domain name,

you'll want to secure it so no one else grabs it first. To do this you will need to purchase it from a domain registrar or web hosting company and you'll usually pay a small fee for the privilege—this can be anything from £1 to £30 ($1.50 to $45) or more per year, depending on the domain and extension you choose. Names registered with the most popular .com extension can usually be purchased for around £10 ($15).

It doesn't matter if you buy your domain name from one of the popular registrars such as GoDaddy or NameCheap, or if you purchase it from a different web hosting company. I tend to register new domains through the same company I use for hosting my websites, simply because it's easier if everything is in one place. Doing it this way also saves you having to point your domain to the host provider's servers later on. I know others prefer to register all domains through GoDaddy because it's cheap, then use a separate hosting company, but the choice is entirely yours.

If you decide not to use one of the more popular domain registrars, be sure to check that your chosen company are accredited by ICANN, the Internet Corporation for Assigned Names and Numbers. This non-profit organisation oversees domain and server registration worldwide and is the globally accepted body within the industry.

Privacy

When you register a domain name, you'll likely be asked if you want to add on Domain Privacy. For me, this is a no brainer to say yes to, because it means that your contact details are protected from the public, and this means hidden from the spammers.

If you turn down domain privacy, you'll probably find your inbox stuffed full with uninvited web design and SEO offers the very next day. You'll soon tire of all these annoying emails so get yourself the domain privacy as soon as you register your domain, then your inbox can rest easy.

With your domain name, you will usually receive access to an email address, which you can start using even before your website is built. This means you have no excuse not to start building your email list and sending out information and offers using your new domain's email address immediately.

Now you have your domain in the bag, it's time to think about how to turn that name into a real live website. To do this, you'll need somewhere on the internet to store your website files, so let's take a look at web hosting.

Getting Hosting

If you've never set up a website before, you may not be familiar with hosting but it's actually a very simple concept.

If you think of your website as a party, you're always

going to need somewhere to throw that party—that's at your host's venue. Your host might live just down the road, in the next town or could even be on the other side of the world, but either way, he's there to serve your guests, make sure your party runs smoothly and look after you day and night.

Your actual web host is simply a set of computers, connected to the internet, where you can store all the files and data for your website. The host leaves their servers permanently switched on, making your website available at any time of day to anyone who visits.

Hosting Packages And Costs

When you go to sign up for web hosting for your website, you will usually be offered different levels of service. This can vary from host to host but in general there will be a basic package where you can put your website on a shared server and have access to all the basic services you would need for a single site.

As you move up through the packages, you will see shared hosting replaced with dedicated hosting, meaning that you don't share your website's server with anyone else who is also renting space from the host. Shared servers *can* slow your website down but when you first start out I would recommend you start with the shared hosting. Then if you encounter problems or grow beyond this server's means, you can always upgrade to more appropriate hosting for your needs.

You do get what you pay for with hosting so it's worth checking reviews that others have left before deciding which hosting company to place your website with.

There is nothing prohibitive about the cost of a website. After purchasing your domain, usually for under £10 ($15), all you need to get started is a basic hosting package. These start at around £3 (under $5) per month, which is insignificant compared to the potential it can unlock for your business.

With any hosting package you should also have the ability to create multiple email addresses for your website. For example, if your website is abc.com, you will be able to create email accounts in the format anything@abc.com. Check with your host provider how many mailboxes are provided with each package.

The good thing about getting hosting is that you can usually upgrade or downgrade at any time, with no loss of service or downtime. So I would advise to start basic and upgrade when necessary.

Where To Get Hosting

There are hundreds of web hosting companies to choose from but you probably don't know most of them when you start out. You may have heard of the popular ones such as Hostgator or GoDaddy but as with any purchase, it's advisable to check out reviews by people who have used these companies before. These big corporations that are most famed for their cheap domain name registrations are not always the best choice for hosting too, so do your research and find one with a good reputation before you invest.

The company I use here in the UK for both my domain registration and web hosting is LCN. I've found they provide an easy-to-use web interface, give excellent customer service and have very knowledgeable and helpful support staff. If you have a technical issue, they'll email you articles while you're on the phone so that you don't have to go scouring their help pages for answers. I'm slowly moving all my websites to be under the LCN umbrella, as they give exactly the service I've been searching for.

I've also used Bluehost for domains and hosting. Bluehost are a United States based company with a good reputation, who I have found provide good customer service and are a popular choice for many of my state-side friends.

If you have several websites that require a more dedicated service for higher traffic demands, LiquidWeb are the go-to company for many. They are more expensive but if you're an internet marketer who has many fingers in lots of internet pies, they may be worth looking into. I haven't used this company so I am only reporting the positive experiences of some of my worldwide colleagues who swear by it.

A Note For Europeans

An issue recently came to light regarding the importance of where your website servers are situated if you are a European business. It would seem that if you host your websites on servers outside of the European Union, there may be a data protection issue. As this law is not yet clear, I recommend sticking to using a hosting company with servers situated in your own country.

Chapter 3: Summary

- **Domains and hosting are very affordable**. The cost should never prevent you moving forwards with your business.

- **Choosing a domain can be fun but you must avoid naming blunders**. Choose a name that has potential for growth in your product range or business expansion and be careful of how it sounds when spoken or if it has potential for misinterpretation.

- **Use online tools** to help you choose a name and check availability.

- **Do your due diligence**. Before you choose a web hosting company, make sure that good service is evident by reading reviews.

Introducing WordPress

*"I don't think of work as work and
play as play. It's all living."*
~ Richard Branson

One of the things I loved about being at school was that
the further into your education you got, the more options
you were given as to which subjects you would specialise
in. For me, this meant tossing out history, biology and
French, and getting deeper into maths, physics and
German. As you figure out what you most enjoy and what
you're best at, these choices become even easier to make.

The same was true on my path to better websites. I started off old-school, coding everything from scratch, which was fine until a world of new possibilities came onto the scene. Although I resisted for a number of years —I was a traditional coder and I wanted to stay close to the coal face—I eventually could not ignore the pull of something shiny and new that the world was embracing. I've never looked back since.

I'm talking about WordPress; the most popular website framework in existence today, with a quarter of all websites worldwide being based on it.

WordPress was originally a place to "press words"—a blogging platform essentially—but it has now grown into the easiest and most widely used framework for website developers and business owners to get to grips with. Using WordPress, you can finally create a masterpiece of your own in record time, without the need for complicated coding.

So let's have a closer look at WordPress, which flavour you should choose and what it can do for you, your website and your business.

I'm No Web Designer!

Let me start by saying that you don't need to know *any* code to design your own website in WordPress. Your site's code is hidden from view to make it less susceptible to human error, and 99% of the time you won't ever need to access it.

WordPress is one of a number of available Content Management Systems (CMS), which make the process of designing content for a website both easier for the end user and also better organised behind the scenes. There are other popular CMS frameworks, including Joomla! (yes, with the exclamation included) and Drupal, but WordPress is touted as being the easiest to implement and understand for those new to websites or having no knowledge of coding.

The benefit of using any CMS is that it provides a way to update content using a simple user-interface, often likened to the ease of using Microsoft Word to create a document. A CMS also allows you to apply site-wide updates that apply to all content instantly. Perfect for any business owner venturing into the online world for the first time in other words.

This all means that WordPress is an extremely user-friendly framework. It's a place where you can quickly get comfortable and where you are not overwhelmed by too much tech.

There *may* be a few learning challenges to overcome, but with a quick overview of the user interface, you can be up and running fairly quickly.

Which Flavour?

Did you know that there are two different options when it comes to setting up a WordPress blog or website?

The first is found at WordPress.com. Here, you don't

need to buy a domain or hosting and you can have a free blog set up in 5 minutes. However, there are a few drawbacks of using this flavour of WordPress. For starters, your URL will be in the less-than-friendly format *www.mywebsite.wordpress.com*, which is a bit of a mouthful and tells the world that you're maybe not as serious about your website as you could be. The other downside of WordPress.com websites is that you can't upload specialist themes or use plugins on your site, which could be a deal breaker if you want a custom look or to add extra functionality.

There are advantages of having a WordPress.com site though—it's free to use, you don't need to worry about hosting, security or updates, and there are still hundreds of themes available for you to use.

If you're just starting out and aren't sure if having a website is for you, WordPress.com is the perfect place to get a feel for the user interface and see how you progress.

Most serious website owners use WordPress.org to build their sites with. This is a free-to-use, open-source community project, with hundreds of developers worldwide contributing to its source code. WordPress.org has evolved from a blogging platform into a full CMS and the possibilities provided by the thousands of plugins are astounding.

The good thing about WordPress.org is that you install it on your own domain and hosting, leaving you in full control and able to tailor it exactly how you see fit. But as you can imagine, with this responsibility also comes challenges, but that's why you're here—to overcome the gaps in knowledge and understanding that being dropped in at the deep end can bring.

WordPress.org is free to use, but you will need to bear the costs of a domain and hosting. With these being relatively cheap, it's a no brainer.

Endless Possibilities

You could be forgiven for feeling overwhelmed by the amount of themes and plugins available in WordPress—there are thousands of each. But what this actually means is that no two websites are ever going to be the same, as it's unlikely that different business owners would choose the exact same theme, plugins, colours, fonts, page layouts and images. This means there is room in the market for everyone to stamp their individuality onto their internet space.

When you first install WordPress onto your site, it will be delivered with a default theme ready to use, which in recent years has been named after the year it was introduced.

The starter theme is great for getting your first few blog posts written and adding a couple of pages to your site. But once you get familiar with things and have a little content under your belt, you'll probably want to explore the huge library of themes. You can then choose one that suits your preferred style, your audience's needs and your functional requirements. In Chapter 7 we'll go through all the considerations you might make when selecting a suitable theme.

There are also thousands of WordPress plugins to choose from, and these little gems can do anything from enabling you to sell digital downloads to adding email opt-in forms to your site, and almost anything else you can imagine. This is where the possibilities explode, but you shouldn't go too overboard adding plugins, especially those you don't really need, as they can slow your site down and occasionally interfere with each other or with your theme's inner workings.

In the bonus download area of the website there is a free download you can grab, which will give you a rundown of the essential plugins I think every site should have. Many of these have become my absolute favourites that I can't live without.

Behind The Scenes

You might not care what goes on in the background when you create a WordPress website but in case you *are* curious, here's the deal in brief.

WordPress has two elements to it:

- **A database** to hold all the data for your site, including blog post and page content.
- **A folder structure** to hold the WordPress installation files, your uploaded media files and also

your themes and plugins.

These two go hand-in-hand and one can't work without the other. WordPress communicates between the files and the database, providing a very organised and efficient working structure.

If you ever connect to your site's files using a File Transfer Protocol (FTP) client, you'll be able to see those file types listed above. All other content is stored in your website's database, hidden from view, and is retrieved only when someone lands on one of your pages.

My advice would be to never tinker with your website files via FTP unless you fully understand what you're doing. You should definitely not experiment with any database changes unless you consider yourself a pro—and even then you should always make a backup first.

One Click Installer

When you choose a hosting company for your website, it's advisable to pick one that offers the One Click Installer for WordPress. It literally does what it says on the tin— you click once and hey presto, within a few minutes your website is installed and online, ready for you to get to work on. If you don't have the One Click Installer available, you will just have to go through a couple of extra steps in order to get your site up and running—your host provider should be able to provide full instructions on how to do this.

Themes

If you're new to WordPress website design, the term "theme" may not be familiar. So what is it?

I like to think of a theme as a set of styles and behaviours. Just like a themed party where everyone knows what type of outfit they should come in and how to act to compliment their look, a theme can be thought of as the glue that makes the party (your website) a cohesive success.

When considering new themes for my websites, I always think in terms of what they can do for my content. I assess the possibilities the theme offers, based on combination of the following three properties:

1. **Style**
2. **Layout**
3. **Functionality**

All three must score highly for me to consider a theme for a development.

Overall style pertains to the way the website will look with the theme installed. The most popular styles are:

- **Blog/Multi-purpose**—the most common website theme type, traditionally used for blogging or general websites that don't need anything over and above the standard pages and posts.

- **Magazine**—used for websites that churn out lots of content regularly. Sites such as buzzfeed.com and bbc.co.uk use magazine style as they want their visitors to have plenty of choices when they visit the home page. Magazine style sites often use guest writers to enable them to put more content up more often.
- **One page**—commonly used for product launches and also for individuals to present their CV on. It literally is a website with one page, usually split into distinct sections as you scroll down. This style can also be used as a landing or sales letter page.
- **Portfolio**—great for photographers or artists to show off images of their work.
- **E-Commerce**—specifically designed with selling in mind. Can usually be used for physical or digital products.

With thousands of WordPress themes available and many of them being free of charge, there is never a shortage of choice. So how do you make that decision? By also looking at the layout and functionality.

When I'm considering a new theme I like to look at the demo site, if one is available. I'll preview all the menu styles, design options and layouts of the pages, the font and colour options, the possibilities for buttons and boxes, how images are displayed, whether it has specialist functionality such as pricing tables or accordion text boxes and so on. I try to imagine all the types of content that I'll be creating and visualise how it would look with the given fonts, image shapes and page layouts. If I think the content *will* suit the theme, it goes into the possibles pile. Or actually into my virtual pile of bookmarked themes, of which there are now many.

There's one property that can kill a theme's viability for me and that's lack of responsiveness. That is to say that if a website made from that theme doesn't rearrange itself nicely when I view it on my mobile, I won't even consider using it. I usually test this quickly by narrowing my browser window to its smallest setting and see how the site looks. Then I'll double check on my mobile. With over 60% of all traffic coming from mobile devices, or even more if you're only driving traffic from apps such as Instagram, it's not even worth considering a theme that isn't responsive.

Having said that, there are plugins available that can turn any site from non-responsive to responsive, but I haven't yet needed to use them so I can't comment on their effectiveness. If you already have a site you like but it's just not responsive, the premium plugin **WPtouch** or the free **Jetpack plugin**'s mobile theme option might be options for you to try.

If you can't find a free theme that does what you need within your WordPress dashboard, or if you want a top notch website with quality design and extra functionality, it could be time to buy a premium theme. Most can be purchased for between £30 to £60 ($45 to $90), which is not too pricey when you consider the potential for your website to make way more than that back.

Some of my favourite places to find premium WordPress themes are:

- **ElegantThemes.com**
- **ThemeForest.net**
- **Mojo-Themes.com**
- **Theme-Junkie.com**
- **ThriveThemes.com**

Out of the above list, Elegant Themes and ThemeForest are my go-to theme sites. Elegant Themes offers 87 gorgeous themes for one low price, the most flexible of all being **Divi** and **Extra**. With these two, not only do they come with lots of pre-defined layout templates to choose from, but if used in conjunction with the Divi Builder, you can design any layout you can dream up. Elegant Themes also offer their own set of WordPress plugins for just an extra $20, so you can cover your email opt-in, social share, mobile friendliness and shortcode needs too. Elegant Themes are constantly adding new features to their themes and plugins, which means they're probably going to be around for the long haul.

ThemeForest.net is part of the Envato Marketplace, where anyone can sell their digital creations. There are hundreds, if not thousands, of WordPress themes available at ThemeForest and the good news is, they all have a working demo of the theme in action. It can take some time to find ones you like, but this up-front research will enable to you hunt out a theme that does everything you want, looks good and is also fast and responsive. Prices average around $45-$60 per theme, which usually includes lifetime updates.

With ThemeForest, it's always a good idea to check the user reviews and look at the support questions for the theme—make sure the developer is answering questions promptly and doesn't have too many bug reports.

Once you've found a theme you can't live without, simply purchase it, download the theme's ZIP file then upload it to your website to get started using it.

Plugins

Plugins provide functionality for your website, over and above the standard theme features. They can be thought of as optional extras, a bit like when you buy a basic model car then choose add-ons, such as the incorporated sat nav or the alloy wheels.

As with themes, there are thousands of free plugins available in the WordPress admin area, many of which are rated highly and offer excellent functionality. There are also many premium plugins, developed by individuals around the world, costing anything from under £10 ($15) to a few hundred.

The good news is that most of the plugins I use and

recommend are free and can be installed with 2 clicks. WordPress makes it very easy to add functionality so even if you have a theme that lacks certain features, you can often add them later.

Essential Plugins

Whenever I install WordPress, there are a few plugins I always put onto my site immediately. Why? Because they are absolutely essential if you want to secure your site, make it run faster, get you found in the search engines and more. One of them also gives me cheaper advertising, which is a good reason to not forget to install it.

In the bonus downloads area, you'll find a handy guide to all the plugins I consider to be must-haves, that I install on almost every website. For each, there's a description of what they do and how you will benefit from using them.

Download my guide,
Essential WordPress Plugins
No Website Should Be Without,
by visiting:
http://crackingthewebsitecode.com/bonus

Chapter 4: Summary

- **Choose a self-hosted WordPress.org website** if you're serious about your business. WordPress.com is restrictive and mainly used by bloggers who don't need extra features or by business owners just starting out.
- **Take time choosing the right theme** for your website. Make sure it's responsive in design and has all the basic features and styles you're likely to need.
- **Install the essential plugins** onto your site as soon as possible, to protect you and give your site a clear advantage.

The 10 Essential Ingredients
Every Website Needs

"People think focus means saying yes to the thing you've got to focus on. But that's not what it means at all. It means saying no to the hundred other good ideas that there are."
~ Steve Jobs

With thousands of themes, plugin functionality, fonts and colours at your fingertips, it's sometimes hard to reign in your creative fire at the start of a project. All of this is important to a degree but nonetheless, there are a few absolute essentials that no website should be created without considering. These should be at the core of any design before you ever put finger to keyboard and it's important to not miss any of these.

You will find the exercises in this chapter available to print out and complete in your companion workbook.

Let's have a look at what these core components are.

1. Defined Target Demographic

Long before you even set out creating a website, you need to know who you are creating it for. You need to get fairly specific on this as if you get it wrong you could end up with a site that appeals to no one, brings in zero sales and is a complete flop.

And no one wants that.

Let me ask you—do you *really* know who your customers are? Do you know how old they are, where they shop, how much they earn and what they like to do on a weekend?

This might sound impossible to know for sure but I bet you one thing—most of your previous customers will have a lot more in common than you think. Or at least they should have if you're doing your marketing correctly and attracting a particular type of client in to your business.

If you're too general in your marketing and try to attract too wide an audience, you can come across as unfocused and people may feel a bit *"blah, whatever"* towards you.

But if you can figure out and define your ideal clients' common traits so that you know exactly the type of person you're trying to attract, you can then be much more specific in the way you market yourself and your products or services.

All of the content you add to your site and all of your advertising must be written with this one ideal client in mind. And I literally mean one single client. When you write or speak as if it's to one specific person, you'll find you attract many more of this same type of person and that's when you'll feel like you're really gelling with your audience. And that's when they'll be more inclined to buy from you.

So how do you get crystal clear on the profile of your ideal client? Simply by putting yourself in their world and writing down everything they would be doing, feeling, seeing, wanting and wishing for. Getting into their mind and understanding their life and worries will give you a real advantage.

Use the exercise below to dig deep into the mind of your ideal client, then reference this every time you design new content or products.

EXERCISE 5.1: Define Your Target Demographic

Write down as many personality and lifestyle traits about your ideal customer as you can. Here are some things to think about:

- Is this person male/female or could they be either?
- What age range?
- Married/single?
- Do they work?
- What job do they do?
- How hard do they work?
- Do they have kids, pets?
- What are their hobbies?
- Are they outgoing or reserved?
- Where do they like to shop?
- Are they extravagant or frugal?
- What do they value in life?
- What lifestyle do they dream of?
- What are their goals in life?
- What are they afraid of?
- What keeps them up at night worrying?
- What problems do they have in the areas of life, work, family, time, money?
- What problems do they have that your business could provide a solution for?
- Anything else that defines this person's life, desires or struggles?

2. Customer Focused Approach

Why do so many entrepreneurs get this so wrong on their websites? They fill up their home page with BUY-ME-I'M-THE-GREATEST-THING-EVER-style offers, long paragraphs of boring, irrelevant blurb and dubious attempts at attention-grabbing sales pitches, when all the visitor really wants to know is:

- **What can you do for me?**
- **Do you have what I'm looking for?**
- **Do I like the look of what I'm seeing?**
- **Do I like the sound of what I'm reading?**

If your site doesn't answer these questions in the first few seconds, the chances are you'll turn off your visitor, possibly for good. Lost at sea with no compass, looking for the exit to the lifeboats is not the way your customers should feel.

In all the above points, you can see that they're all focused on what you can do for your customer, not the other way around. Keep this in mind constantly as you decide what's in and what's out on your site.

Your content, especially that on the home page, is your introduction to what you can offer, and first impressions count tremendously. If you met your potential customer in person, you wouldn't go in hard and try to dazzle them with your most expensive show-stopper of a product right away. You'd be more likely to woo them gently with your unenviable knowledge of your niche. You'd find out more about them and show how you can help solve their most pressing problems. You'd be friendly and offer them advice and solutions before you showed them the price tag to anything.

So why not take this approach on your website?

Try to design your web pages in a way that draws your visitors in, give them the answers to what they're looking for, lets them know they're in the right place and guides them deeper to discover more.

In short, it's *not* about you, so keep that in mind.

3. Overriding Strategy

Do you have a strategy? What's your ultimate goal for a visitor to your site? And what are the baby steps that you want to take them through in order to get there?

Your strategy must be at the forefront of your mind when creating your website. Without one you might as well be peeing in the wind. In fact, that might be more productive.

To execute your strategy well, you need to first think of the end goal—what is the ultimate outcome or action that you want a visitor to take? I assume that you know the answer to this—whether it's to buy products from you, sign up to your coaching program, join your online course or whatever else you have in mind. But you must define that end goal. Setting up a website without it will feel a hell of a lot harder as you won't know what you need to have in place and you'll probably waste time on things that won't bring you closer to where you want to be.

Let's make up an example. Say you have a Big, Fat Coaching Program that costs £1000 ($1500). Ultimately you'd love your customers to sign up for this program. That's your dream and desire. But how do you get someone who comes to your site to get their wallet out to the tune of a grand?

I'll tell you what you *don't* do, and that's try to sell them the £1000 baby straight off. If you do, there's only one way that's going to go—down like a lead balloon. You'll probably lose that potential customer forever if you try to bully them into spending big bucks from day one— no one likes to be railroaded into spending a fortune when they're simply not ready.

Your strategy must therefore be reverse engineered from the end goal backwards. You need to identify all the steps that a visitor could go through before they sign up to your top priced offering.

In this example, before someone buys your ultimate coaching program, they're probably going to want to sample some of your other products first, to weigh up the value you deliver and decide whether you're a good fit for them.

So how do you get someone to commit to these smaller items? The easiest way is by delivering great content and real value to them first, without trying to sell anything.

Once you've warmed up your potential buyer, you can then test if they're ready to commit to something smaller by offering them a low priced item. Once they're a buyer, you can then work your way up to your higher priced offerings, providing more and more value in between, with no strings attached. Some call this process walking up the ladder of value, but however you look at it, it's most common to start the customer off with a small purchase and build up incrementally to that ultimate outcome.

Of course there are exceptions to this step-by-step approach, such as if you're a furniture retailer and only sell sofas, you're probably not going to try to coax shoppers to sample just a cushion first. But, assuming you do have various levels of entry to your products or services available, let's continue.

To get your visitor to the end goal, you need to identify the enabling steps along the way. In the coaching program example, these may look something like this…

1. **Get visitor to website**
2. **Visitor signs up for free download**
3. **Visitor downloads free item**
4. **Visitor receives a series of emails containing interesting and relevant information**
5. **Visitor is offered low priced product(s)**
6. **Visitor buys product(s)**
7. **Customer continues to receive emails to build value and trust**
8. **Customer is offered the high-end coaching program**
9. **Customer buys coaching program. END GOAL REACHED!**

(Note: in all the excitement, don't forget about the delivery of the purchased program to the client, that's a step I shouldn't need to spell out!)

What I've just laid out above is the journey that someone new to your site may go on over a period of days, weeks or even months.

When they buy your big fat coaching program, that's not really the end of the road, you'll still continue to send them great information on a regular basis and if anything, you'll send them extra special gifts for being one of your top clients.

You should always have a long term strategy so that you can identify the smaller steps you need to take to make the next action in the sequence easier for your customer to swallow.

Once you break your goals down into smaller, practical steps such as those outlined, it makes the task of implementing each one much less daunting. It's also more manageable both physically and mentally. Once you can map out and see your path to success like this it will feel less overwhelming and you're more likely to tackle it head on, one step at a time.

EXERCISE 5.2: Define Your Strategy For Fulfilling Your Ultimate Goal

What's the ultimate end goal or action that you'd like your ideal client to take? Write out the steps of how you will get a new visitor to take that action, starting with

the ultimate goal at the bottom of the page and working backwards.

Work back up to the top of the page, identifying each previous smaller step of the process that you may need to take your visitor through, in order to turn them into a highly qualified paying client.

If you have more than one end goal, for example if you have two programs that suit distinctly different audiences, write out a strategic sequence for each one— there may be different steps and outcomes depending on where you're aiming to end up.

4. Supporting Functionality

Once you have mapped out a strategy that will turn a regular website visitor into a customer and potentially into your best paying client, you need to be sure you have the right functionality in place to handle it.

Using the big fat coaching program example above, you must next identify the functionality you will need to employ, so you can fulfil each step. Looking at the sequence of steps above, we can identify that we need the following functionality:

1. A way to bring visitors to the website
2. A way to collect email addresses
3. A way to create some lower ticket products
4. Page(s) on the site to showcase products for sale
5. A way to allow purchase of products

6. **A way for the buyer to download or be shipped products**

7. **A way to send a series of follow up emails automatically**

8. **A way to deliver coaching to the customer**

Once you can break down your processes into functionality like this, you'll have a much clearer idea of what you need to do both within your site and also what supporting tools you need that extend beyond your site, such as an email autoresponder or paid traffic.

EXERCISE 5.3: Identify The Required Supporting Functionality

Go back over the strategy you wrote out in the previous exercise and identify all the elements of functionality that you'll need to have in place in order to enable each element of the strategy to be implemented.

5. The Non-Sexy Stuff

Outside the sales process, other functionalities that are essential for your site are backups and security. These are not sexy and don't offer any visible enhancement to your site but they are an absolute must.

Without protecting from hackers or technical failure, you'll leave yourself wide open for potential problems or total loss. We'll look at safety and security in more depth in Chapter 12.

There are other types of functionality that your site may benefit from and these are often niche-specific. For example, you may want to use a recipe formatter if you run a cooking blog.

EXERCISE 5.4: Identify Specialist Functionality
Identify any other specialist functionality you might need and add it to the list you made in Exercise 5.3.

6. Kerb Appeal

Whenever I talk about your site being appealing, I don't mean *to you*. I don't care if it appeals to you and neither should you. You're designing your site for your target audience and your target audience alone. If they don't like it, you're doing both your visitor and yourself a disservice.

Realise that not all sites benefit from being beautified with pretty pictures, swirly fonts or over-the-top design elements. Often it's the simplest designs using a single highlight colour and showcasing a few selective areas of interest that are the most intriguing and visitor-worthy. There is no one-size-fits-all definition of appealing, and that's why you need to again refer to your target demographic, and design your site with *their* tastes in mind, instead of your own.

As an example, if the visitors coming your site are predominantly male, aged over 50 and are into guns and battle reenactment, the chances are you're not going to want a bright, colourful site with feminine overtones. In this case you might consider something that's very masculine, functional and to the point; something that focuses on the imagery of guns and war, and allows the visitor easy access to your latest articles, battle reports or gun reviews. This set up might not have kerb appeal to much of the population but it will appeal to those who matter, and that should be all that you care about.

What your visitor wants to see and how they want to see it must be what you focus your efforts on. If your site design doesn't grab their attention, guess where they're going? Somewhere else. That's a huge shame and it's something that could've been avoided if you'd thought more about your audience and designed your site appropriately.

Creating an appealing design doesn't require an expensive team of designers—far from it in fact. By choosing the right theme for your site, using carefully selected colours and layout options and building in the required functionality, your site should appeal to the person it was designed for. And everyone else who doesn't like it can bog off, because they're not your target audience and your site is *not* for everyone. Remember that.

We'll look more in depth at how to make your website better looking in Chapter 7, but first let's make sure you can identify what your ideal customer would like to see on your site, by answering the following questions.

EXERCISE 5.5: Decide How To Give Your Site Great Kerb Appeal

Look at your description of your ideal client and put yourself in their shoes. Imagine coming to your site for the first time and think about what you would want to see. Write down answers to all of the following questions:

1. What colours does this person resonate with?
2. What specific language, words and terminology do they use when talking about their struggles or desires?
3. What type of imagery appeals to them?
4. Do they like plain or fancy? Subtle or bold? Warm or cold?
5. What type of brain stimulation most appeals? Visual, mental, auditory?

7. Responsive Design

Making your website look good and function well on mobile devices should be at or very near to the top of your list of website requirements. You only have to walk down the street and observe how many people are nose-to-the-ground, with their eyes on their mobile phone screen instead of on the path ahead.

On average, around 60% of website traffic comes from mobiles and tablets, so it's not worth annoying over half of your visitors with a poorly executed design, unless you're ok with the same amount of potential profits going down the pan too.

When a site is truly responsive, the elements on the page, such as images and buttons, should automatically rearrange and readjust to fit smaller screen sizes and you should not have to zoom in to be able to comfortably read the text. Once your site is able to be viewed easily on all types of devices, your *potential* audience satisfaction goes back up to 100%. And who wouldn't want that?

To check if your theme is responsive, simply bring up your website on your mobile or tablet device. If you have to use your zoom capability to be able to read the words, it's probably not responsive. If the images go off the sides of the screen, it's probably not responsive. And if the various elements on the page don't shift around and arrange themselves neatly down the page instead of across it, it's definitely not responsive.

When designing your website, picking a theme that is responsive is the easiest way to ensure you never have to worry about this issue again. If your theme is programmed to adjust image sizes, text areas and design elements on the fly, all you have to do is worry about creating good content.

That's the ideal, but there are a huge amount of themes out there that don't fit into this category. So if yours isn't responsive to begin with, what can you do about it?

The first option is to install a WordPress plugin that converts your site to be responsive. I can't claim these type of plugins work 100% of the time but they're touted as being very capable. As it's just a plugin, you can install it, check your site on your mobile and if you're not happy, just remove the plugin and try another solution.

The second option is to swap your theme to a responsive one. It's an option but I know what a pain it can be to swap themes, especially if you've spent time adding customised styling, so if you're happy with your current theme, try the plugin route first.

EXERCISE 5.6: Ensure Your Site Is Responsive

Check out your website on various tablet and mobile devices and look to see if it displays well. If you have to zoom in to read text or use horizontal scroll bars to move across the screen, it's time to put functionality in place to make your website responsive.

8. Pertinent, Quality Content

Think back to the last time you landed on a website that took you aback and you thought, "Wow, they really get me, this is exactly what I've been looking for". It doesn't happen often, but when it does, it's something you remember for a long time.

One of the last sites that did this for me was my mentor, Vicky Fraser's. There was something about the words on the page that grabbed me from the outset, that made me want to read more, that I really identified with. The more I read, the more I wanted to read. She spoke to my inner being in language that resonated perfectly with my core beliefs and values. The content was relevant to me and—even better—the timing was perfect.

Interestingly, the reason I ended up on Vicky's website was through a Facebook ad, so she obviously had her targeting spot on too.

Imagine if every visitor that landed on your site had that same experience; if what they saw was something so perfect for them that it was as if it was speaking right to their hearts; if you were able to deliver that to your visitors, do you think your conversion rates would go up? I do.

And that's what having pertinent, quality content is all about. It's about speaking the same language, writing in such a way that both answers your reader's deepest wishes and calms their biggest fears. It's about creating something that can move them and give them exactly what they're looking for at the right moment.

Practically, you can't give every single visitor everything they want all of the time, but what you can do is give your ideal visitor solutions to the problems they most commonly have. And when you can identify these and create content to suit, that's when your website becomes captivating like Vicky's was for me. The interesting thing is that Vicky's website is very simply designed. No clutter or distractions. Each page serves one purpose and one purpose alone. This is the type of focused approach that can get a visitor hooked in no time.

9. To Be Found

What I'm talking about here is your site's ability to be put in front of your potential customers just at the right time, and that time is when they're searching the internet for exactly what you have. You can create the most beautiful, fully functional site in the world, but if no one ever lands on it, its existence is pointless.

When you create your site, its find-ability, if that's a word, can be enhanced by a number of factors. These include using good SEO (Search Engine Optimisation), effective use of keyword phrases within your site's pages and smaller details such as the file names you use for your images. We'll cover all the details of this topic in Chapter 9, but just know that if they can't find you, they can't buy from you.

10. Regular Content Updates

If you're building a simple one page website, created with a single purpose in mind, and you're sending paid traffic to it, updates are probably irrelevant. But for everyone else, the importance of updating your content regularly can't be stressed enough.

For most small businesses, updates to your website are a good reason to ask existing customers to pay a return visit, and of course this can introduce new opportunities to buy from you.

Links to new content can be sent out via an email

newsletter, on social media or even via text message but the important thing is to get your links out to as many people as you can.

If you use good SEO on your blog posts (see Chapter 9 for more on this), you'll increase your chances of being found organically, often by people who haven't seen any of your content previously. Getting new visitors to your site is incredibly important, as each one provides a fresh opportunity to begin the path towards getting a sale.

Putting out updates doesn't mean that your previous content is dead however—far from it. If you write blog posts on topics that don't go out of date—often referred to as evergreen content—you can share links to these at any time in the future or repurpose the same content into many different formats, giving you plenty of write-once-use-many-times content.

Building up a large content library on your site is certain to boost your chances of being found in the search engines, so make sure you set time aside each week to write at least one new piece of content. Make sure it's relevant to your target audience and if you can make it something they've been asking for, you've a much greater chance of a boost in traffic and sales due to shares and interest in your topic.

All actionable exercises in this chapter can be found in the Companion Workbook, at: http://crackingthewebsitecode.com/bonus

Chapter 5: Summary

1. **Know your audience.** The most important activity before you do anything is to hone down who you are designing your site for. Get your customer clear in your mind.

2. **Customer first, you second.** Remember that your website is for your customers to use and enjoy, so make it work for them.

3. **Identify your strategy.** Get those big goals clearly defined and the mini steps for how to get there.

4. **Get the right tools for the job.** Tools, functionality, ways to help you execute your strategy—know what they are and get them in place.

5. **Stay safe.** Put a good security and backup solution in place to protect you from those tricky hackers.

6. **Draw people in.** First impressions count and no one likes to look at an amateurish website. Make it appeal to your target audience members by using words and design elements that appeal to those exact people.

7. **Be responsive.** If your stats show that mobile users are visiting your site, you need to make sure your site is responsive so as not to annoy the pants off them.

8. **Be Relevant.** Stick to the point and only include information relevant to your audience and niche.

9. **SEO—healthy not stealthy.** Make sure you get your SEO right and use keywords that have a good

chance of getting you found in Google.

10. **Write often.** The more relevant content you can add to your site, the more reasons there are for people to visit.

How To Avoid Looking
Like An Amateur

*"Those who are blessed with the most talent
don't necessarily outperform everyone else. It's
the people with follow-through who excel."*
~ Mary Kay Ash

Let's face it, we all start off as amateurs. In fact, an amateur could be defined as someone who does not get paid for their hobby or pursuit. Professionals, however, are the people we all look up to, aspire to be like and envy, because they are masters of their trade and usually earn a tidy sum for doing so.

So what sets you apart from the professionals when you start out creating your website? Experience is the first trait, knowledge is quite possibly another. Ideally, there would be a way to fast track your way to the higher end of the scale in both of these areas, and that's what this chapter is intended to go some way towards.

Below are the solutions to some of the most common mistakes those new to web design often make. Taking action on these points will quickly enable you to graduate to beyond the amateur stage, so take note and take action.

Begin With Purpose

People love a good design. When The Eiffel Tower was commissioned, it was to be the main exhibit of the Paris Exposition of 1889. Its purpose was to commemorate the centennial of the French Revolution and to demonstrate France's industrial prowess to the world.

But which do you think came first for the tower—the purpose or the design? The answer of course is the purpose—after all, how would engineer, Gustave Eiffel, have known what to design if he hadn't been given guidance on the purpose of his work? Purpose *has* to come first, or the design will be pure guess work.

The same principles and order of events should apply to your website. Often it's the look and feel of a website that's considered first, because it's so easy to think in terms of colours and pretty layouts. But without knowing the reason for the website's presence, how can you even begin to suggest how it might look or function?

Yes, the excitement of a shiny, new website can take over your thoughts. You might dream of the elements that will make your site visually appealing, but a great website design can never outdo one that is purpose-built and created with a specific outcome in mind.

Be intentional.

If you're still not sure about the purpose of your website, go back to Chapter 5 and read the section entitled Overriding Strategy. Identify your end goals and work out how you will achieve these. I bet you'll see that none of the steps that make up your strategy can be achieved in the first instance by dreaming up a fancy colour scheme.

Know Your Customers

In the place I grew up, you could often walk through the town centre on a Saturday afternoon and be approached by scruffy looking guys, trying to force a leaflet into your hands. Free drinks before 10pm at the latest nightclub opening, big discounts at a previously unheard of furniture store, cheap tickets to the circus matinee—the offers were completely random.

The problem with this type of indiscriminate mass-marketing is that the take-up rate is incredibly low. Lower than low in fact. Without pre-qualifying someone to see if they're right for your offer, how do you know they even have *potential* to be interested? This thoughtless methodology annoys those being approached and makes them want to do all they can to avoid the guy on the next street corner waving another pile of uninteresting print.

If you apply the same unfocused approach to marketing your website, all you'll do is spend a fortune on advertising to the wrong crowd and probably end up with just a handful of less-than-ideal website visitors. But if you can tune in to who your customers are, where they hang out, what their problems are and how you can solve them, you'll attract more of the people you want to work with or provide solutions for. Knowing your target audience demographic is imperative.

If you didn't do the exercise to define your ideal customer profile in Chapter 5, please go back and do this as soon as you can. You won't be able to write relevant content or design your site for your customer if you don't know who they are.

Me, Me, Me Syndrome

When I was young, my mum used to whisper to me, "I love me, who do you love?". She wasn't being vain, in fact she wasn't talking about herself at all. She'd say this when she noticed someone openly bragging.

The fact is that people do love to talk about themselves and be the centre of attention, whether they care to admit it or not. And it's not limited to when things are going well —people also love to share their disappointments and struggles. In these moments, it's all about me, me, me and personal validation is what people crave. The empathy received from a friendly ally can help someone feel understood and important again.

So when it comes to designing your website, don't let it be all about you. Keep it focused on your customer and design it solely with them in mind. And if you're not sure what they want, here's a shocker of a suggestion—ask them! Send them a survey, talk to them in person, phone or email them, but be sure to find out what they are struggling with and what type of solution would help them the most. Then simply focus on providing what they need.

When it comes down to it, what *you* like or want it is completely irrelevant. If you hate your site but your customers love it, you have the potential to make sales. If you love your site but your customers hate it, what have you got then? Simply a self-indulgent website that does nothing for your business. I know which I'd choose.

EXERCISE 6.1: Determine What Your Visitor Wants To See

Put yourself in your customer's shoes. Imagine you've never visited your website before but arrive on it for the first time. Answer the following questions to help you get clear on what should feature prominently on your site.

1. What are some of the main reasons a client would visit your site?

2. What types of content would interest your client or provide solutions for their needs?

3. Identify anything on your website that doesn't fit with any of the above and either move it to somewhere less prominent or lose it completely.

Be A Good Tour Guide

There's one mistake I see so often, see if you can relate.

You're on a website and you scroll down the page and —nothing! You've come to the end of what you were browsing but there's nothing to tell you where you can go next—no suggestions of what else you may find interesting, no direction whatsoever. So what do you do? You leave.

If you've designed your website well, your visitor will be able to take cues from you as to what to do next. For example, at the end of each blog post, you would do well to include either an opt-in form for your email list or suggestions of which related pages and posts on your site your reader may also find interesting. You can do both of these very easily and it could make all the difference between someone reading one page on your site then leaving, and staying browsing for longer and potentially becoming a subscriber or customer.

One of the main places people look for guidance is the main menu of your site and they will look for that at the top of the page, so make sure that's where it is. Use a font that's easy to read, make sure all your most important and most popular options are visible on the first level of your menu, and ideally don't have more than one level of sub-menu if you decide to use a dropdown beneath the top level menu. If things are too difficult to find, people tend to give up and go away.

It's sad to say that even fully grown adults need to be hand-held and shown what to do next. So if you're not providing an easy path to discovering other parts of your site, you could be losing valuable business all too often.

EXERCISE 6.2: Be A Good Tour Guide

Have a look at your web pages and see if you're providing an easy transition through your content. Make sure you have the following in place:

- **A menu structure at the top of the page that has all your most popular options visible and available with a single click.**
- **Clear calls to action at the end of sections, pages and posts to take the reader to where you want them to go next.**
- **A subscriber opt-in box underneath blog posts to encourage sign up for your mailing list (with opt-in bribe if possible).**
- **Hyperlinks within your articles for quick links to other pages on your site.**
- **Call to action buttons wherever you want to ask your visitor to take action—make them bright and obvious.**

- **Graphics that draw the eye towards content you want the reader to notice, such as your sign-up form or special offers.**

Sell The Benefits

Features and benefits. Do you know the difference? And most importantly, do you know which one you should sway more towards in your marketing?

When you describe the features of your product, you're essentially just naming the cold, hard facts. There are usually no feelings associated to the features of a product, so listing them is not what will get you the sale. All your visitor will know is what it does, not what it can do for them.

Start describing the benefits and you're now into the realms of selling. Benefits evoke emotions that can cause your customer to attach themselves to potential improvements owning your product could bring.

In short, banging on about benefits rather than the features should be your number one selling technique. You should definitely state the features in your pitch too, but these are only there to back up the benefits and provide a logical reason to complete the purchase.

As an example, if you're promoting a recipe book and you just concentrate on listing its features rather than any of the benefits, your description may look something like this:

New cookbook with 50 recipes, full colour photographs, macronutrient counts and step by step instructions.

It sounds okay but it doesn't necessarily make you want to get your wallet out does it?

But if the we add in the benefits of each feature, the description becomes much more appealing and we can imagine how this book might help us achieve our goals and live a better life.

Look how it reads after including the benefits:

Brand new cookbook with huge choice of 50 recipes so you never get bored of the same old food, full colour photographs so you can see what mouth-watering dishes you're about to eat, macronutrient counts so you are in control of your weight and don't have to worry about over-eating or calorie counting ever again, and step-by-step instructions so you don't have to think about a thing and you can simply concentrate on entertaining your friends and enjoying yourself.

The difference between the first description and the second is the use of emotional triggers, which stimulate the imagination. Notice that for each feature, I added the phrase "so you" before I described the benefit. If written effectively, benefits can pull on the heart strings and are more likely to sway people towards a buying decision than a stark list of features alone.

So when you're writing your web pages, emails or advertising copy, always try to get the benefits across to your readers first, as they are more likely to be hooked if they can get an answer to the question, "What's in it for me?". Once you've got their attention, you can back up the benefits with all the amazing features your product has. Of course, don't forget to ask for the sale too.

Remember, people buy primarily based on emotions and then qualify or justify their buying decision by falling back on the facts.

EXERCISE 6.3: Sell The Benefits

1. **List the features of one of your key products or services.**

2. **Now go back through your feature list and next to each, list a benefit you know your customer would gain from each feature.**

3. **Visit your website and reword the description for this product to also reflect the benefits to your customer, as well as telling them about the features. Use bullet points where appropriate, for easy reading.**

4. **Go through all your product pages and make sure you are talking more about benefits than features, rewording each item description if necessary.**

Don't Let Anyone Leave Without Action

I'm not suggesting you can hold people hostage on your website, but there are many ways to keep them browsing for longer or get them to return in future. If your site has good content and appeals to your visitor, you should make sure they know that you have more to offer.

It's a good idea to have an incentive scheme for your website, whereby a visitor can hand over their email address in return for something of value. This could be a free report, a mini course, a coupon for their next purchase or simply the promise of some great future content. Whatever your incentive is, it must have a perceived value to your clients or they won't take the bait.

It's very easy to put an opt-in form on your website in various locations, to capture email addresses with. We'll go through the options for doing this and which are the most effective in Chapter 11.

Once you have your visitor's email address, you'll have the advantage of being able to follow up with more information, education and of course offers. Without this means of following up, all you have is a website that visitors arrive at and then leave. Building relationships with those who have visited is the best way to convert them from one-off browsers to regular customers or raving fans.

Start thinking about what would be valuable to your customers. What could you give them in return for their email address? It could be a checklist, cheatsheet, printable item, ebook, mini course delivered via email, links to some great tools or resources, a video showing how to do something. There are so many options but just be sure to create something useful to your website visitors and get your follow up emails in place. Your giveaway doesn't have to take too long or be too extensive. Think more nutshell than novel.

We'll go deeper into opt-ins, giveaway bribes and email marketing in Chapter 11, so hold that thought for now.

Realise The Need For Speed

If you didn't catch on to this fact already, we're living in an age with a huge demand for information to be served at a lightning-fast pace. This unfortunately means that even a two second delay when loading your web page could have your visitors hitting the back button and abandoning ship before they've even seen your home page logo.

To keep your website running at optimal performance, make sure to:

- **Remove any unused plugins.**
- **Keep your image sizes the smallest they can be by uploading them at the size they're intended to be used at, and use an image optimiser plugin. I'll talk more about the specifics of image sizes in the next chapter.**
- **Install a caching plugin on your site, to help**

speed up access for returning visitors. This will enable image-heavy pages to load faster, as the visitor will already have a copy of those images on their device, saved on their previous visit.

You can use a website speed tester to find out if your website is sluggish, such as the one at: **http://tools.pingdom.com/fpt/**

If your pages are shown to be slow to load, take a look at the ideas above for improving the situation. Implement one idea at a time then retest to see if you've cracked it.

Don't Let It Fester

I have to make this point because too many business owners seem to think that getting a website live on the internet is the end of the story. They go through all the pain and hard work of setting everything up, and then—nothing.

Creating your site is akin to the start of a tender growing process—if you don't water the plants, they die off. Same goes for your website.

You could create the most stunning website that initially gets you some attention, but you run the risk of gaining very little else from it unless you make regular updates. Just imagine how likely *you* would be to return more than once to a website if all you ever saw was the same old content every time.

People are glued to the internet these days and they're used to the speed at which new content comes up in their social media news feeds. They want to be entertained and made to feel good by what they see, so if your content is static or boring then where's the incentive to come back? I'm afraid there isn't one so please take a look at your site from a visitor point of view and ask yourself if it's eye-catching and working for you—i.e. bringing in leads and sales regularly— or if it's simply sat there gathering dust. Is it interesting enough for you to stay? Be honest and impartial if you can.

If yours is a website that visitors are likely to want to return to in future, at the very least you should change your prominent home page features frequently to pique interest for return visitors.

A great way to make sure you don't forget about your site after you create it is to use a publishing schedule. You can simply print out a month-to-a-page calendar, such as the one I created for you in the bonus package, and fill in the title of the content you will create on the days you intend doing so. Other than being able to see how a whole month's content will play out, the other advantage of using a content planner is that you are more likely to stick to it if you treat each entry as an appointment with yourself.

Your printable Monthly Content Calendar and Companion Workbook can be found here: http://crackingthewebsitecode.com/bonus

Chapter 6: Summary

1. **Define your purpose up front.** You can't design your perfect website unless you understand the purpose of having it.

2. **Figure out who your customer is, quickly.** If you skip this part, you won't know who you're designing your site for and that could be costly in the long run.

3. **It's not all about you.** Keep your website focused on your clients' needs—it's not your pet project.

4. **Provide clear signposts.** People need to be told what to do, otherwise it's human nature to do nothing.

5. **Talk up the benefits.** Mention the features for sure, but make sure your sales pitch is all about what your product can do for your customer.

6. **Lock the exits!** Or at least ask your visitor to give you their email address in exchange for something useful before they leave. This is your key to a more profitable future via relationship building.

7. **Speed matters.** Make sure your site loads quickly by saving images at the appropriate size and allowing caching.

8. **Don't give up.** Once you have your fabulous site up and running, keep it updated with new content and tell people about it often.

Ways To Make Your Website
Better Looking

*"Your brand is what people say about you
when you are not in the room."*
~ Jeff Bezos

It's said that you only have around seven seconds to make a good first impression. With a website I'd put that down to around three. In this digital age, your website has to get its worthiness across quicker than ever.

How good your website looks is not just about what colours or fonts you use, it goes much deeper than that.

Many of the notions of what makes a website attractive are not easily quantified in words and can also be subjective. But let's take a slightly more formulaic approach, looking at all the features of a website and how they can best be used to give an overall look and feel that gratifies and makes a great first impression.

Go Theme Shopping

If you're in the early stages of creating a web site, you may not yet realise the value in using a premium web template for your site.

Think of it like buying a car. You can go for the basic on-the-road model that will get you from A to B perfectly well, or you can go for the higher specification with the heated seats, headlight washers, chrome trim, metallic paint, active suspension and 4-wheel drive flip switch. The upgraded model also gets you from A to B with no problem, but it does three extra things—it looks more attractive, probably performs better and it has all the functionality you need. With a premium theme you're left wanting for nothing if you choose carefully, keeping your specific functional requirements in mind.

Although there are some free themes on the market that are very good to work with, you'll usually find that the one with all the bells and whistles has a fee associated with it. But this fee is relatively small and usually worthy. Most come in around £50 ($75), which over the lifetime of your website is quite insignificant.

There are many advantages to buying a premium theme. For a start, they're more likely to have been written with the latest coding standards in mind and be kept up-to-date often. This is important as it guards against potential incompatibility problems when updating the core WordPress functionality. With a free theme that comes with little or no support, when things start to go wrong, you may have no choice but to swap themes, which is always a pain in the neck as you will inevitably have to redesign some pages and set up your new look and feel options as a minimum. If your premium theme developer is reputable and keeps their code up to date, you're less likely to have this type of issue later on because the updates will integrate into your current design seamlessly.

Another reason to invest in a paid theme is the extra functionality they often offer. Free themes tend to be fairly lightweight in the amount of control you have over page layouts, menu options and styling, whereas premium themes tend to go the extra mile and offer the ability to change multiple features at the click of a mouse. If you find yourself feeling limited with your free theme, it's often this lack of flexibility that's holding you back.

Back in Chapter 4, I gave you a list of sites I recommend you purchase premium themes from, but wherever you source yours, be sure the designer provides regular updates and doesn't have too many unfavourable reports in his or her support forum; protect yourself against future problems as much as possible.

De-Clutter

How many times have you gone to a website and just not been able to find what you're looking for? One of the problems some site owners suffer from is a type of hoarding, where they'll just throw everything they can think of onto the home page, in the hope that their visitor will somehow find what they need.

Sometimes that chance will not come around because frankly, your visitor will get bored or frustrated before they get to that nugget of information they were looking for. This only means one thing—the exit crosshairs.

In order to improve your website's navigability and ease of use, try to organise your pages with categories that your visitor can delve deeper into, rather than overwhelming them with too many choices up front. Don't get me wrong, choices are good, but give people too many and you'll probably scare them off. Most people don't have enough staying power to figure out your site, so make the job easy for them. Get rid of anything that you wouldn't want to be clicked right off the bat and think in terms of what content will keep your visitor clicking and reading, rather than buzzing off to YouTube to watch more cute kittens.

Be More Like Mona

Let's face it, Lisa—she of Mona Lisa fame—wasn't particularly stunning. The term enigmatic is widely used to describe her look and it insinuates that you can't really tell what she was thinking or feeling. She had something about her that you couldn't put your finger on; she was mysterious. And this is what made the painting so intriguingly successful.

If you apply the same logic to your website, it's that little extra something that you maybe can't put into words, that makes someone hang around for a longer look. So by that token, does this mean your site has to be drop dead gorgeous? Not necessarily. It just has to have *something*, and that something has to appeal to *your* target audience.

So how do you make sure your website does that? It's all about:

- **Sticking to a consistent set of fonts and colours as your base for all content**
- **Carefully choosing images, words and design elements to provoke interest and curiosity**
- **Having the right components in the appropriate and expected places**

Just like a patchwork quilt, there are many ways to put these pieces together, but some designs turn out more successful than others. Often, only experimentation will help you see what works and what doesn't but there are some basics of design that will help you achieve a coherent look faster. Let's now have a look at each of these, so that you end up with an enigmatic Mona Lisa and not a horrific Scream.

Pick A Colour Scheme

Grey. Think of that for a moment. And I don't mean Christian of *50 Shades* fame.

From the name of that one colour you can start to conjure up images—dark clouds, muted scenery, a sombre mood. Colour is a powerful method of evoking emotion and it can certainly affect how people feel about your website when they visit, so think carefully before plastering your site with that hot pink you so love. Ask yourself if your customers will love it too.

There are theories behind how different colours make us feel and what emotion we associate them with. Blue is said to be a sign of security and trust, which is probably why so many websites use it for their accent colour in headings, buttons and images. Green is said to be the easiest on the eyes and is often used to help us relax. Not surprisingly, pink is thought of as romantic and feminine, often being used to market products to women. Luxury, strength and power often are associated with black, whereas orange is a colour people link with taking an action, such as clicking a button, as demonstrated and implemented so perfectly by Amazon.

Interestingly, both men and women tend to favour blue and green, making these the most popular colour choices for highlight colours on websites.

You may have a colour or set of colours in mind for

your site, often based around your logo or set of core images but if you're open to discovering a new colour palette, try out Adobe's Colour Wheel tool, at:

https://color.adobe.com/create/color-wheel

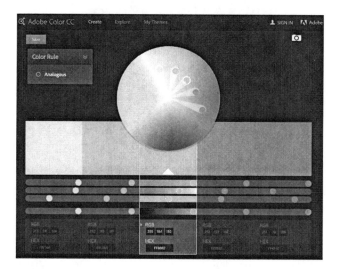

By sliding the fan of fingers around the colour wheel, you can quickly obtain the colour codes for a set of colours that either match, contrast or blend well together. You can then use these on your website when creating buttons, links, backgrounds and image overlays.

Alternatively, if you have a particular image that you love the colours of, you can upload it to:

http://lokeshdhakar.com/projects/color-thief/

Dominant Color

colorthief.getColor(image).rgb

Palette

colorThief.getPalette(image).rgba

This clever little tool will extract the colour palette from your photo and give you the dominant colour in the image and all the secondary colours. From here you can decide which of the colours you want to use on your site—ideally no more than 3 or 4—and you can screenshot the colour palette to pick up the colours in your photo editing tool, or send it to your graphic designer if you have one.

Use Typefaces Consistently

The same rules apply to typefaces (often referred to as fonts) as to colours. If you want your website to appear professionally designed, choose no more than two or three complimentary fonts and stick to them throughout.

Sans Serif styles that are plainer in nature tend to work better for a website's body text as they are easier read on computer screens. Examples of this are:

Arial

Helvetica

Calibri

Open Sans

For headings you can allow yourself a bit more freedom and flair, but make sure that the style you choose is clearly readable at all screen sizes.

If you like the style of text on a particular website you visit, you can discover what is it with an online tool called Fount, found here:

http://fount.artequalswork.com

Drag Fount's bookmarklet to your browser's bookmarks bar, then click it when you're on a website you like. Fount will display the typeface, size and style in the top right of your browser.

Another way to discover free styles to use on your website is by going to Google Fonts:

https://www.google.com/fonts

I like to use this tool to find a suitable font for my website headings and with that in mind, you can type in one of your typical blog post headings in the field at the top and see how all the different styles look using that text. This makes it much easier to visualise it as if it were on your website, as shown in the next picture:

Choose Quality Images

Selecting high quality images for your website can really help it look professional and give the impression of it having been expensive to create. Whether you use images to showcase your products or just as incidentals to make your blog posts more interesting, they *will* get noticed. It's up to you to make sure they're as good as you can possibly make them.

What makes a good image can be subjective but one thing is for sure—bad images stand out a mile off. When I talk about bad images I mean those that bear no relevance to the related story or product, photos that look like they were taken by a two year old child, or imagery that isn't consistent with the rest of the website's content.

The great thing about using captivating images on your site is that it will open up even more avenues where you can showcase your work. On image-sharing sites such as Pinterest or Tumblr, a great image could be seen and shared hundreds or even thousands of times, each share potentially leading someone back to your website.

The images you choose should be a reflection of the message you're trying to convey. They should also be relatable—if your audience immediately feels affinity towards them and understands the story you're trying to convey with the image, you'll know you chose well.

If you can make your graphics visually enticing, you could quickly multiply the traffic to your website with a few strategic shares on image-heavy social sites.

When creating graphics for your website, ask yourself:

- **Does the image help me get my message or point across?** If not, change or remove it.
- **Does the image fit with my overall style?** Consistency and cohesion are key to your overall visual effect, and images play a huge part. Many sites use coloured overlays or a particular style of lettering on top of their images, but whatever you do, keep the style going throughout.
- **Does the image shape match those already in use on my site?** If you are displaying a portfolio of featured blog posts that include a thumbnail picture, it's a good idea to make sure the featured images you upload have the same height and width ratio each time. If you stray from this, your blog

roll can look a little disjointed or out of line, which can detract from the consistency of your site.

What Size Should Images Be?

There are two meanings to the term image size. The first refers to the width and height dimensions and the second, the file size. Both are important.

You want the images you use on your website to have the smallest file size possible, for the height and width you are using, so they don't slow down your page's loading speed. To reduce file size, you can save an image at the same width and height, but at a lower resolution, or you can reduce the width and height dimensions and keep the higher resolution. Web images should be at least 72 dots per inch (dpi), but no higher than 300.

The width and height are often referred to by the number of pixels (px). Here are some guidelines you can use for the dimensions of images, for various uses:

Image Type	Suggested Width
Thumbnail	200-300 px
Sidebar Image	300-400 px
Blog Post Featured Image	600-900 px
Full Width Image	1800-2000 px

The sizes in the table above largely depend on the layout of your website pages. If you have a sidebar then you will have less space in the main body of the page, so your images can be slightly smaller.

If you consider that the average width of a standard web page is around 1000 pixels, you can usually determine the approximate size an image needs to be, to fill the allotted space.

On mobile devices, the screen resolution and size is much less than on computer monitors, but as long as your site design is responsive, it should adjust to suit all device types automatically.

Assuming you have saved your images at the most appropriate width and height for their target placement on your site, you then need to consider the size of the file on disk. If you go to your file explorer and see that your image is 2Mb in size, this could take a few seconds to download to your visitor's browser, which is possibly too long to bother hanging around for. So when you upload an image to your website you have two choices of how to make sure the file size is optimal.

The first option is to save the image as small as you can, without losing quality, before upload. This can be done in a photo editing program such as Adobe Elements, Photoshop or Lightroom, using the "Save for web" option and selecting a lower value of image quality in the output settings. You can also use free image editing programs such as RIOT, Gimp or pixlr to do the same job.

The second option is to use a WordPress plugin such as **Imagify** or **WP Smush** to optimise your images as you upload them. With this type of plugin, you can be sure your website will not suffer from performance issues due to image file sizes but your images will still display in high quality.

I like to go all in and create the smallest images I'm able using Photoshop to start with, and also use a plugin on my websites to provide a final touch of optimisation. Some may call it overkill, I like to call it making sure.

Where To Find Good Quality Free Photos

I have a few favourite places I regularly curate photos for my websites from. Here are a few to get you started:

- **Pexels - pexels.com**
- **Unsplash - unsplash.com**
- **Pixabay - pixabay.com**
- **PicJumbo - picjumbo.com**

All the above sites offer completely free photos and usually include the right to modify and use the image as you see fit without even crediting its origins. But make sure to check the licensing for any free photos you use.

Another place to find images is by using Google search, but you must be careful with this method as most images that come up in the search engines can *not* be used freely elsewhere. Even if a photo does not state its copyright, it is implied by law, so using photos found on Google is likely to get you into legal hot water if you are found out.

If you do want to find photos using Google, the best way to hunt down copyright-free images is to type your search term into Google, click on Images, then click:

```
Search Tools -> Usage Rights -> Labeled for
reuse
```

This will show you images that *in theory* are allowed to be used by anyone. But this method is still not perfect and it's always best to check with the original author if you want to use their photo on your own site.

Premium Photos

If you're creating blog posts or social media status graphics, I don't believe you need to pay for exclusive images to get your point across. However, the trouble with using free stock photos is that everyone else is doing the same, so if you don't put your own twist onto the graphic, such as altering the colour profile or overlaying some stylish text, your images are probably going to appear elsewhere too. It's like turning up to a party in the same dress as someone else—shock horror! In some people's opinion, this could devalue your work and make you less original, but if you can accept that this is going to happen at some point, just use images as you find them and don't worry about it. I don't believe in wasting time on small details if they're not directly going to increase your bottom line. And touching up an image where the original is perfectly acceptable is probably not one of those worthy activities.

If you're working on a larger project such as an original eBook or an advertisement for your new product, you'll probably want to upgrade your graphics and go a little more exclusive. If you're not someone who can create their own unique images, this is when premium stock photos are a godsend.

The quality and variety of photos, graphics and even video that you can purchase from stock photo agencies is incredible. I've never failed to find just the right image that I was looking for on stock photo sites such as iStockphoto.com or shutterstock.com. Prices currently work out at around £8 ($12) per photo, or more if you go for one of their high-end options.

Premium photos can be worth the investment if you want to create high quality designs that stand out from the crowd. But once you've downloaded your paid-for images, it's important to compliment them with professional graphic design. Don't panic if you've not much natural talent in this area, there are ways you can make things look professional, even if you're clueless.

You may be pleasantly surprised by the array of online design tools available today. The reality is that you can create great graphics on a budget, or for free in many cases.

Borrowing ideas from other people's designs is an option, but with that comes the danger of copying too closely and being accused of ripping someone else's idea off. So let's not go there and instead let's look at some online design tools that help you create exactly what you need without too much skill and zero copying.

Design For Non-Designers

Canva is a fantastic online design tool, found at canva.com. Within Canva you can design your own professional-looking graphics for anything, including Facebook ads, infographics, posters, presentations and even multi-page eBooks. They have a huge range of templates to choose as a starting point and if you don't have your own photos to use within your chosen layout, they'll even provide stock photos for $1 each. Here are some of the design templates you could start working with in Canva:

With this fabulous array of designs and styles, you never again need to use the excuse, *"I'm just not creative"*. Canva have done the hard work for you, all you have to do is put your words and pictures into the pre-designed templates and you have a fabulous-looking image or PDF you can download and use in your content right away.

Easy Infographics

Infographics are also in vogue right now because people seem to love statistics—that's facts and figures—presented in picture form. If you can present complex information in a simplistic manner, more people will look at it and also understand it. Infographics appeal to the masses because of their eye-catching draw.

Don't worry if you don't own any graphics programs for your computer, the online tool, PiktoChart, can make your statistics look impressive in no time.

At piktochart.com you can create graphics and poster-style images that work perfectly with your data. Start with one of their templates and add your own words, icons and pictures to make it into something quite unique. Shown below are some of the free starter layouts that PiktoChart provides. You'd be proud to create something like this wouldn't you? Try it out, it's good fun and people will be genuinely impressed with your efforts. And of course they'll want to share, which again means more traffic to your website.

With the amount of free images and tools available, you've no excuse for having crappy photos or graphics on your website, or anywhere else for that matter.

Chapter 7: Summary

- **Use a premium web template or theme.** Such items are very keenly priced and can transform your site from distinctly average to very-definitely-professional within a few clicks.

- **De-clutter.** Keep your pages tidy and free from lesser quality items, to keep your visitor focused on what you *want* them to see.

- **Choose a suitable colour scheme.** Sticking to a pre-defined colour palette will not only make everything feel more consistent, but it will enable your visitor to recognise your content more easily.

- **Stick to 2 or 3 fonts.** Choosing one font for your body text and another for your headings is about as complicated as you need to make it. Use them throughout and you'll give your visitor a better experience.

- **Use quality images.** With thousands of free images available online, there's no excuse for poor quality graphics. Overlay text for a unique piece of content.

- **Get to grips with online design tools.** With such easy opportunities to create stunning graphics, you'd be mad to ignore them.

Increase Your Earning Potential By Writing Better Copy

"The most powerful element in advertising is the truth"
~ William Bernbach

There's a reason good copywriters command large fees—they're worth every penny. If you can master even a fraction of what those who get paid thousands know, you could see a significant increase in your response rate and therefore your earning potential.

I've spent the last couple of years learning everything I

can about writing good copy, learning from some of the world's best and implementing it in my own websites and emails. I'm still watching, analysing and learning every day, it's an art form that you can never know enough about.

The best copywriters are a dab hand at sending subliminal messages to our brains through their use of Neuro Linguistic Programming (NLP). A simple sentence that looks perfectly innocent might actually be giving your brain the cue to take immediate action, without you even realising it. Brilliant copy can even make you believe it was your idea in the first place. But you don't need to be a master NLP practitioner to better your writing. You can improve what you put down on the page just by implementing a few basic ideas, which we'll look at next.

I don't claim to be a guru of copywriting by any stretch, so my tips here are what I've picked up and implemented with a decent amount of success on my own and my clients' websites and emails. If you want a more in-depth look at copywriting, I suggest reading a specialist book on the subject or taking a course. My mentor, Vicky Fraser, is one of my favourite badass copywriters and I'd highly recommend her *49 Ideas* series to get you started. It's available for free on her website at vickyfraser.com

It's important to stress that you don't have to be a writer to write. I'm not a writer by trade but yet here I am, having written this book full of thousands of words. Over 43,000 words actually. We all have to start somewhere and just because you've never written articles or emails before, that's no reason not to start.

To grow your business, you're almost certainly going to have to create content in some form, so don't stress, just take these few simple tips on board then get started.

Write Perfectly Well, Not Perfectly

Any content you write does *not* need to be absolutely perfect. If you're the sort who will go over every little detail and rewrite sentences that are already good to go, you'll waste time and never publish anything.

The secret is to know when you've done enough to get your message across with no obvious bloopers, and not obsess over the tiny details that might make it 1% better. Ask yourself if you're likely to lose customers if you don't spend that extra half hour making things perfect, or conversely if you'll gain any of the undecided if you *do* put in the extra effort. The answer is that probably neither of these things will happen. Being perfect won't suddenly make people love you all the more, just as making the odd little slip up won't lose you a ton of custom either. Everyone is human and it's ok to be fallible. If it's good enough, it's good enough. Stop editing and get the content out there. Unless it's the headline. Now that *does* matter.

Then She Made Me Do *This*

The headline, together with the first line or two of content are *the* most important elements of any content piece. Many of the best content marketers report spending 80% of their time on the headline alone, as it's so crucial to getting your reader interested enough to venture into the rest of your content. If this is true, wouldn't you want to make sure you had the attention of your reader right from the off?

When you saw the sub-heading to this section, you probably wondered what on earth I was talking about—Then She Made Me Do *This*—you might have wondered what was *this* and who is *she*? It's that type of curiosity that gets your readers to continue on to your main content.

Not all headlines have to be obscure or surprising, they can also be solution-based. This format can be extremely click-worthy if the headline is written to address one of your target reader's concerns or desires.

It's a great idea to use solution-based titles (headlines) for your blog posts. If you can write headlines that are used as search terms, you will likely get better results in terms of organic search traffic to your site.

For example, a basic headline that someone may type into a Google search can often be improved for marketing purposes. Take the following example:

How To Get A Flat Belly

This headline suggests that answers to the question being posed would be forthcoming if you read this article, which is fine. But an even better headline would suggest not just answers to the question, but also potential benefits or a way to avoid a common pain point. For example:

How To Get A Flat Belly Without Doing Crunches

This expanded headline not only promises answers but it also delivers a a winning blow. I mean, who wouldn't want to get a flat stomach if you didn't even have to do crunches? The potential benefit together with avoidance of a pain point gives a great headline. This formulaic approach can be repeated for many different sources of angst that your audience member is likely to feel.

Finally, to make sure your headline is one that will attract a good volume of organic search traffic, it's worth using Google's keyword planner tool, which can be found at:

https://adwords.google.com/KeywordPlanner

With this tool, you can research the popularity of any phrase you are considering using as a keyword for your blog posts. You will be able to see if it has a high enough number of searches each month—anything over 1000 is ideal—and how stiff the competition is—that is, how many articles are already out there in cyberspace, using that keyword. If you try to use keywords that have high competition, you may *never* find your post anywhere near the top of the Google search results. But, if you find a keyword or phrase that has a good search volume but low competition, that's a great one to include in your blog post, and is one you *could* more easily rank highly for.

EXERCISE 5.7: Create Your Own Click-Worthy Headlines

To create some attractive headlines for your content, first make a list of all the questions your ideal customer has. Next, make a list of all the pain points they feel about their current situation. Lastly, write out any positive outcomes and benefits they may feel if they could overcome those problems.

To create your headline, pick out one of the items on your list of questions or one of the pain points and pair it with one of the beneficial outcomes your ideal customer can expect to gain. You've got yourself the beginnings of a headline that will entice your readers to want to read more. It will also have a greater chance of being found in the search engines if you research the types of questions people are actually searching for.

Use Google's keyword planner tool to research the popular search terms for your niche and choose terms that have low or medium competition and a good monthly search volume.

Practice writing headlines that address a question or pain plus a desired outcome and start using these as your blog post titles.

So What? Speak To Me!

I'd estimate that around 95% of website home pages follow the standard template of showing a logo, a main picture or sliding set of images, a bold tag line, then a summary of the latest and greatest blog posts. Sometimes, this may be exactly what the person visiting your site wants, but most often it's probably not.

Dig deeper into *why* people visit websites and you'll find that what they *really* want to know is what you can do for them. I'll reiterate what I said about the importance of having a customer-focused approach—people are somewhat selfish in nature, being interested in what you can do for them, not how great you or your products are. Not initially anyway.

So it's not always appropriate to show off your best products or fantastic range of articles, you need to think carefully *why* that person has come to your site, and let them know you can help with that.

Speaking in your visitor's own language, down to the exact phrases they use when they're talking about their frustrations or their desires, is one way to make them feel like you're on their wavelength and understand their needs completely. Listen to how people describe the struggles they're having and learn to mimic what they say in your copy, also adding how you can solve it.

As an example, changing the tag line on your home page from something that describes what you do (*how self-indulgent!*), into something that describes what you can do for your visitor (*so much more appealing*), can be a game-changer. Consider these two tag lines, either of which you can probably imagine being written in big letters at the top of a home page:

1. *Hi, I'm Mark, I'm a financial advisor, specialising in home repossession.*

2. *Scared of losing your home? I'm Mark and I can help you get your finances in order, so you can secure the future of your home and your family.*

Can you see how the first tag line just leaves you saying, "So what?". It doesn't really help the reader learn anything, apart from that Mark is probably highly qualified to do his job. If you ever write a piece of copy that leaves the reader thinking, "So what?", there's always more you can add to qualify it or dig deeper into the benefits, so make sure you do.

The second tag line speaks directly to the reader, first addressing the pain point by asking a question about their current situation. Internally, when you're asked a question, it's really hard for your brain not to respond with an answer, even if you don't say it out loud. This internal, "Yes", from those who need Mark's help, is an example of good copy at work. It also lets those who have come to Mark's page looking for something else, to see much more quickly that this is not what they're looking for, and leave.

This is all good news for Mark as he'll only get those truly interested in his services to continue reading, and not waste his visitor's time if they're not a good fit.

As Mark goes on to describe how he can help someone potentially fix their nightmare situation, relating it to a brighter future, this rounds off his hook nicely and draws the reader in to find out more about what Mark has to offer.

Buying Decisions

If you're struggling to get new subscribers or sales from your website, there's a good chance your copy needs some attention. It can be frustrating to know you have a great product or service, yet still not be able to reach the people who you know it could benefit.

You first have to understand how people make buying decisions, and this goes back to the point I made in Chapter 6 about wrongly promoting the features instead of the benefits. Getting your head round this concept early and applying it to your existing website content can really make a positive impact.

When you ask someone why they bought a product from one website and not another, their answer is often not purely based on price. They might say, "I just liked that site better". What they're actually saying is that the website they bought from was more captivating, maybe reeling them in by focusing on the benefits of the product more than the features. Even though the same product may appear on two different websites with the same images, it's how the details are presented that makes the decision more straight forward for the buyer.

If you've done your research, you'll probably have the right products or services available at a price that your target audience will be comfortable with. But how do you go from having something great to offer and seeing poor results, to having customers queuing up to get on your waiting list? By fine-tuning what you have and sticking to a set of proven principles for all your content.

Let's look at more techniques you can use for maximum impact and more sales.

Write In A Style Relevant To The Context

You may have noticed that different styles of writing are used for different situations. For example, when writing emails for a marketing campaign, they're likely to be better received if the sentences are short and easy to read. Paragraphs are usually kept to no more than 3 or 4 lines long to help keep the reader's attention and make them feel like they're progressing quickly through the email.

When writing blog posts, the content may need a more in-depth explanation and therefore would suit longer paragraphs. Blog posts also lend themselves to the use of bullet points, extra sub-headings within the copy and sections of block quotes. Variations in style helps to break up the monotony of pure text blocks, giving the reader a far more enjoyable experience.

For published items such as eBooks or printed materials, the content usually needs to be more grammatically correct, especially if the audience is looking to it as a source of expertise.

Tailor your content to the context it's being written for and you should see a better response rate because your reader will feel more comfortable with the style presented to them.

One Idea

If you're not sure how best to make your content flow, just think of each paragraph as being there to explain one idea. As soon as you start wandering onto the next topic, that's your cue to start a new paragraph. Writing in this manner will split your content into natural sections and your reader will find it easier to separate ideas.

Of course, if you find yourself going on for more than around a dozen lines, see if you can split your paragraph into smaller sections by looking for points where you pause naturally when reading it out loud.

Dot Dot Dot

In emails, I like to use "..." on the end of one line, to indicate that the reader should continue on to the next line. The "..." creates suspense and is a clever way to ask your reader to continue onwards, without actually asking.

An example of a good use of "..." might be:

It was amazing how quickly they formed a queue…
Oh boy, was I embarrassed!

The first line sets up a mini cliffhanger with a natural pause at the end, the dots asking the reader to continue to the next line to find out what happened next. The second line finishes off the sentence. It's a trick that many marketers use and it works, so try it, but remember it's more suited to chatty-style pieces.

Add Your Personality To Everything

To enable your readers to get to know you better, it's good practice to write in a conversational style, just like I'm doing in this book for much of the time. I would bet that if I read this book out to you, it would sound much like my natural way of speaking. In fact, I hope you are getting a good feel for the type of personality I am by now.

Personality comes across in buckets, even on the written page, as long as you allow it to flow naturally. So don't write like a robot and get all unnecessarily formal, simply write how you speak and your readers will get to know the real you a lot sooner. Keeping this going consistently will result in familiarity and trust, which is a great starting point for bringing in future sales.

Attention, Value, Benefits, Offer

If there was ever a quick way to summarise the format

of an effective piece of writing, this could be it. In four short steps you can win over new customers, just by following this little formula.

First, grab the attention of your reader with a great headline and first paragraph. Then, build value into your message by giving away useful information or sharing links to relevant website content (mostly yours, rather than someone else's that is). From that point you can start to introduce the benefits of your product and finally, put the offer on the table for what you have.

There's no secret behind this technique, it works because you are starting by getting to know your potential customer long before you slap that offer in front of them. By that point, you will have warmed them up to the possibilities that your product can truly help fulfil their needs.

This method does not all have to be put into a single piece of content, it may best be suited to being spread over a series of blog articles or emails. With each additional message, the reader is brought closer to your final offer.

Chapter 8: Summary

- **Write well but don't obsess.** Get fresh content out there and don't be anal over every last detail, people will forgive the odd typo. The exception is if it's a formal piece—get that wrong at your peril.
- **Headlines matter.** Spend time crafting your headlines as these can draw people in or turn them off in an instant.
- **Does it pass the "So what?" test?** If your content doesn't deliver an obvious benefit to the reader, rewrite it until it does.
- **Create with your audience in mind, always.** People are me-centric—they only want to know how you can help them, so make sure to deliver.
- **Write in context.** Know the style of publication you're writing for and deliver what's expected.
- **Split content at natural break points.** Use of paragraphs helps your reader to make distinctions and put pauses in the right place.
- **Add personality in buckets.** Help your audience warm to you by writing in conversational style.
- **Attention, Value, Benefits, Offer.** Keep this cycle of messages going and you'll be on track for a winning campaign.

Tips To Get Your Content In Front Of The Right People

"It's kind of fun to do the impossible."
~ Walt Disney

If you've ever spent hours writing what you thought was the most well-thought-out blog post ever and hit Publish, only to hear crickets, you're not alone.

It's a common misconception to think that presenting a well-written piece of content to the world will automatically net you a big influx of visitors. Good content may get you *some* attention over time but you have to work much harder to be certain of increasing your website visitor numbers and subsequently your ability to attract new subscribers or sales.

Let's look at how you can boost your website's potential readership.

Share, Share, Share Again

So you created some great content, you published it to your website. Now what?

Your main aim should be to get people to see it, read it, enjoy it, share it and hopefully take action. You did remember to put a call to action at the end didn't you?

Let's get your content out there and being seen. First of all, copy the URL link of your latest web page or blog post and share it on all your social networks and inside niche groups that you feel the content would be helpful to. Also share it on professional networks such as LinkedIn and Google+ if the content is appropriate—not everything is suitable.

Using a URL shortening service such as that provided for free at bitly.com also enables you to track where visitors landing on your page came from, which is always good to know. By examining your traffic statistics, you may notice traffic arriving at your website from certain places you shared content but maybe not from others, so you can step up your marketing on the more successful platforms to keep your momentum going.

If you use great images as part of your content, you can also Pin these images onto one of your Pinterest boards. People often browse Pinterest when they are looking for inspiration for upcoming purchases, which gives you all the more reason to make the most of its potential. Here are a few facts that might convince you to try Pinterest if you haven't already:

- **85% of all Pinterest users are female**
- **87% of Pinterest users say they have purchased something they discovered while Pinning**
- **The average order value of sales coming from Pinterest is $50, which is higher than any other major social platform.**

With stats like that, Pinterest can't be ignored and has to be worth trying if you are strong with your visuals and can include a good headline, description and call to action within the image.

Images can of course also be shared on all the social media platforms but are especially suited to places such as Instagram, Facebook, Twitter and Tumblr.

If you like to create video content, make a short teaser clip and share it on Instagram, Vine, Snapchat, Facebook, Twitter and any other platforms you have a presence. Use appropriate hashtags with each post for an extra boost of organic traffic. Provide a link from the clip to your website, giving a reason or incentive as to why someone should bother clicking through.

Of course, the main place you want to put video content is YouTube. Even if you haven't made a film in the traditional sense, you can record slideshows of the main points from your blog posts using screen capture software. or just get on camera and talk through the post. Focus on the benefits to the viewer and put a strong call to action near the end of the video and you should see more traffic to your website, especially if you make full use of relevant keywords and tags within your YouTube settings.

Finally, don't forget to embed your YouTube videos onto your website, this will get you extra brownie points for rankings with the search engines and will also bump up your video view stats on YouTube itself, giving you more chance of being discovered over there too.

Retargeting

All this manual sharing takes time but it's made worthwhile when you're enjoying extra traffic to your website. In order to capitalise completely, there's one extra step you can take.

You know how weird it is when you've been browsing a website, then all of a sudden the exact site or item you were looking at earlier appears as an advert in your Facebook feed? That's not a coincidence, that's what's known as retargeting, and is considered to be one of the most effective forms of advertising. The good news is that you can do this with your website visitors too, with just a few extra steps.

To initiate the visitor capture process, you need to install Facebook's Pixel code onto your site. Once in place, this will place a marker against every visitor to your website and is what will allow you to later advertise to those same people with a Facebook Ad campaign.

The pixel—a small piece of code obtained directly from your Facebook page's Audiences page—needs to be placed into the header code of your website. You can obtain this from the following URL (make sure you're logged into Facebook first):

https://www.facebook.com/ads/manager/audiences/ manage/

Once on that page, go to **Tools-> Pixels** then **Actions->View Pixel Code.**

Adding the Facebook pixel manually to your WordPress theme's header code is not recommended, unless your theme supports additions to the header outside of the underlying theme code. If your theme doesn't provide a friendly interface to add code to the header, you will need to dig into the Appearance Editor to access the header.php file. This is not advised unless you know what you're doing, but even if you do, you will lose any changes you make to this file as soon as your theme is updated. For that reason alone, this method of adding the pixel code is not recommended.

One way around this is to use a child theme, which allows you to keep changes to the styling, header and footer code, even after you update to a new version of the theme. But for ease of use and to avoid having to create a child theme (if you don't already have one), there is another way. I'd recommend using the **Facebook Pixel** plugin. This is a premium plugin but you can download it for free from my bonus downloads page. With this little plugin installed, all you have to do is paste in the Facebook pixel code and you're done. Visitors will then be recorded, ready for retargeting.

Be Persistent

Once you've shared your brilliant new piece of work, don't make the mistake of stopping there. Do you think that every single person in your social network saw that post you just put up? Of course not. So don't be afraid to share it a few more times. Fast moving platforms such as Twitter can take extra shares more often but on slower-moving feeds such as Instagram you'll probably want to wait at least a couple of weeks to re-share, depending on how often you are posting and how quickly your older content slips off the bottom of your feed.

Automate It

We don't all have hours on end to spend sharing our fabulous content over and over, so let's look at how to automate it or at least save some time.

One method would be to install a WordPress plugin on your blog such as **Revive Old Post**, which will automatically share your old content to some of the popular social networks, on autopilot. Simply set the sharing interval, connect to your social accounts, then just sit back and wait for the free traffic.

Another way to cut down the amount of time you spend sharing is to use one of the many social media sharing apps. With these online tools you can upload a week or even a month's worth of content and schedule it to go out at the exact times and dates you specify.

One of my favourite tools is **HootSuite**, which allows you to schedule posts to Facebook, Twitter and Instagram ahead of time. If you have 3 or less social accounts to post to, it's free to use. At the time of writing, Instagram doesn't allow automated posting but what HootSuite will do is send you a reminder when your Instagram post is due to go out, and it will place the photo into Instagram and the text into your paste buffer, so that with another couple of taps you can have your latest Instagram published.

Another tool I've had great success with is **PostPlanner**. This one goes a step extra by allowing you to pre-plan your own content but also to find other people's posts in your chosen niche that have had great engagement. If you want to grow your fanbase on Facebook for example, you can schedule some of the suggested viral posts to be published in between your own posts, giving you some real leverage and your page the sense of being a cool and on-the-ball place to be.

The last tool I'll mention is **SocialOomph**. Championed by one of the queens of social media, Kim Garst, SocialOomph allows you to create several "buckets" of content and run each one on a different schedule. For example, you might have a bucket containing tweets about all your free eBooks; you might schedule a post to be published from this queue twice a week.

You may also have another bucket full of tweets with links to your blog posts, which you schedule to go out once a day. As your blog content grows and you keep adding your posts to this content bucket, the less often your old posts will be shared, meaning your followers are less likely to see duplicate content.

SocialOomph has a plethora of other features including automated following of accounts and follower clean up. It's free to try for 7 days and is definitely worth looking at if you already have a good amount of content you can add straight away.

Pay To Play

There is one source of traffic that can be completely frustrating and totally hit and miss if you're not clued up, and that's the paid variety. From Facebook, Twitter, Instagram and LinkedIn Ads to Google AdWords and solo ads (that's paying to send an email to someone else's list), there are many ways to throw a lot of money away fast. I say that in a light-hearted way but, sadly, it's also true. If you don't know the first thing about advertising on all these pay-to-play platforms, the time to learn is *before* you spend any money, not during or after.

There are whole books and some extremely expensive courses on all these types of advertising, because the topic is so deep and forever changing. What worked last year or even last month may not work today, so try to keep abreast of the latest methodologies and algorithms for your chosen advertising platforms.

If you think about it, it's kind of ironic how you can spend a fortune learning how to *avoid* spending a fortune, but people do. I have, in fact.

There are a few simple rules for advertising that will go a long way to getting you started on whichever platform is right for you, here's a brief rundown.

- **Know your target audience and exactly where they hang out**. If they're 18-20 year old girls they're probably not going to be primarily focused on LinkedIn (no offence to any 18 year old girls that are—respect to you!), but they *are* likely to be found regularly on Instagram and Facebook.
- **Know your competition**. In order to place successful advertisements, especially on platforms such as Facebook where you may specify a set of interests that your prospect has, you need to know who you're up against. Why? Because your target

audience is likely to be hanging out over there too, so by targeting those who follow your competitors' pages or brands, you're more likely to get some interest in yours.

- **Create your best click-worthy headlines**. If you're paying for ads or clicks, you want to make sure to catch your prospective customer's eye. You can do this by using direct shout outs to them, for example, *"Football Dads! Teach Your Son To Play Like Ronaldo Today"*. This example headline also uses the basic headline formula of promising a beneficial outcome, and that's that their son could become as nifty as a legendary player.

- **Speak in the language your audience uses**. If you're really going to get a good click-through rate from your ads, you need to put yourself in your target customer's shoes and speak how they speak. If you've picked up any phrases that come up over and over when you talk to people about their frustrations or problems around your niche area, use these in your ad description. By using the same language, your audience will identify with you and be more likely to click.

- **Use colourful pictures**. Images are often what makes or breaks an advertisement. In split tests, where the same ad is created with the same target audience but using different images, there will usually be a clear winner. This can *only* be down to the image if that's the only difference in the two ads. I've often found that colourful images with a happy vibe about them do better than black and white or neutrally-toned images. Which leads to the next point.

- **Split test everything.** I know it can get expensive to run ads and you may not have much of a budget when you first start out, but in order to learn what works and what doesn't, you must split test to find out. As in the example above, try to only change one variable at a time when split testing, so that you know which alternative got the better conversion rate. You only need to run two parallel ads for 24-48 hours to see which is getting the best results, then you can simply turn off the losing one and put more into the winner. As well as your image, you could also test alternative headlines, different call-to-action wording and variations in description.

Analyse And Adjust

However you get your content out there, it's always important to track where the resulting traffic comes from, so that you know which platform brought you the best visitor numbers. You'll be able to do this more easily if you have a Google Analytics tracking code installed on your website. If you haven't got round to getting this done yet, do it today, it's not too tricky and could prove insightful.

By analysing your visitor stats and their sources, you

will get an understanding of which platforms are reacting best to your content and which format or topic is getting more traffic. Once you know these statistics for sure, you can then plan to create more of what's doing the best for you, then share it with your most responsive audiences.

Rinse and repeat.

SEO Everything

As important as creating and sharing content with your existing audience is, it's always nice to reach new people with your content. For those people, *all* your content is fresh and who knows, you might have the exact answer they've been scouring the internet for.

You may get some organic traffic but you can give yourself a big leg up on the search engine rankings by using good SEO throughout your site.

What is SEO? It stands for Search Engine Optimisation and good SEO represents a set of easily implemented guidelines you can apply to each page and blog post on your website, to boost your rankings in the search engines.

Within a WordPress website, one of the most highly recommended plugins that will help you achieve good SEO on your content is the **Yoast SEO** plugin. Once installed, it will tell you what you could improve on each page, to increase your chances of being found. It's one of the most useful tools you'll ever install, so get it today if you don't yet have it. Then make sure to use it to its full potential by taking heed of its recommendations.

Here is a quick summary of some of the ways you can improve the SEO of your pages:

- **Use a title of at most 70 characters**, because anything after that won't show up in the search engine title preview.
- **Use your title again** in the first and last paragraph of your blog post of page and put it inside a H1 or H2 tag somewhere on the page (that's a first or second level heading if you're not familiar with tags such as these).
- **Set the focus keyword** to be part of the title of the page.
- **Add a meta description**—this is the short paragraph that will show below your post title in the search engines. It should provide an overview of your post and include a call to action to encourage clicking, which in turn tells Google your post is highly relevant and gives it a boost in the rankings.
- **Use your focus keyword 3 or 4 more times** throughout your post, but make it read naturally— Google is not stupid and will penalise you if you vomit the keyword anywhere and everywhere.
- **Name your images** the same as your post title before you upload them.
- **Use an Alt tag on your images**, which also contains the focus keyword.

- **Use short paragraphs** and don't use a long word when you can use a shorter one — ease of reading is key.
- **Write at least 300 words** on each page or post.
- **Include hyperlinks** to other articles on your site and/or links to articles on other websites within your post.

If you follow at least 50% of those suggestions for improving your SEO score, you should gain a few ranking positions quite easily. It's worth going back over old posts and seeing how you can make these small improvements, the bonus being getting your content in front of even more people.

Use A Good URL Structure

The Permalinks setting in WordPress determines the format of your blog post URLs, and this really does matter, so listen up.

You may have just done a double take on the previous paragraph. Perma-what?

When you install WordPress, the default format of the URL given to each blog post is pretty useless, looking something like this:

http://www.mywebsite.com/?p=123

That ?p=123 on the end there doesn't give you any clue

as to what the blog post is about, so it's of no use whatsoever. The search engines also can't gain any useful information from this type of URL, meaning you may end up way down in the rankings and no one will see your brilliant post.

This is where Permalinks settings come into play. In WordPress, you get to choose exactly how your blog post URLs are made up, so I'd invite you to ditch that ugly style above and instead include your blog post title in the URL.

This can be done by changing the Permalinks in your WordPress Settings area. Set it to "post title" for maximum exposure in the search engines.

To go one step further with this SEO hack, you can also include the category in the permalink structure, giving the search engines even more information about your content, and potentially getting you a higher listing. If you want to go this extra mile, you can set your permalink structure to:

/%category%/%postname%/

I will put a small disclaimer on this technique—as Google and the other search engines are always changing their algorithms, using the category as part of your permalink structure may or may not give you an SEO boost, so my best advice is to research what's working today before jumping in with this.

Plan And Execute

Content creation can feel like a bit of a chore, unless you plan ahead and take control of it. That's where having a content creation plan comes into play.

Imagine sitting at the computer, wondering what to write about today and getting that stuck feeling again. How would it feel if you had a plan of action set in advance and all you had to do was execute it? It would be a relief I'm sure.

A content creation plan doesn't have to be complicated. It can be as simple as an A4 sheet of paper, divided by 2 criss-cross lines into 4 sections. Think of each section as a week and then start adding titles and ideas to each one.

Another way to plan efficiently is by adding content titles to a month-to-a-page calendar. By doing this, you can quickly see what you need to be doing to get all your content ready for the next month. Plan 2-3 months in advance and you never need panic about having nothing to write about again. You can download my free monthly content planner in the bonus area of the website.

If you want to produce one blog post per week, add an idea for each week's post to your planner. If you want to write an email series or a lead magnet, split the overall content into sub-headings and place these in different day's content boxes. Just keep doing this until you have ideas for a whole month or more.

Now when it comes to writing this content, you can either do it all in one day then take the rest of the week off, or maybe plan to create for an hour, three or four times a week until it's done. Use your time wisely to enable you to get your content out but not be chained to the computer all day.

Once you've got everything created in advance, all you have to do is either schedule WordPress posts to go out at the time and day you prefer or put your email series into an autoresponder sequence, ready to go. You get the idea —plan ahead so you know exactly what you're supposed to be doing when you get to the computer and be as efficient as you can. Content creation will then stop being a chore and will be something you execute with ease, because you have foresight and feel in control.

If you own a seasonal business, you may need to create content many months in advance but if you apply the same principles of planning and creating ahead of time, you'll never have to worry about running out of ideas or time, or facing the blank page again.

Make A Content Creation And Sharing Plan

How much time should you spend on content creation? This is not an easy one to answer as it usually depends on the answer to the other question—how much time do you have available? Or more precisely, how much time are you *willing* to devote to content creation?

If you have a blog and are driving traffic to your articles, one post per week is usually manageable, maybe two or three if you have more time on your hands or if you want to build your business quicker. Other, more time-consuming content such as a whole new email series or an eBook will take you longer to create but the rewards from it could be far greater. So if you're short on time or can't *make* time for more than one good piece of content per week, always choose the one that is going to bring you the best returns.

It may be that you need a set of blog posts written before you can send out your email series that refers to these posts, so you can't do one without the other. Only you will know what you can manage and what should be higher on your priority list.

But think of this—if it takes you two hours to write a blog post and half an hour to craft a new email for your autoresponder series, could you use the two and a half hours that you might spend watching a film on a Sunday night to do both of these for your business instead? If you can make another productive couple of hours mid-week, your site content will be growing in no time.

Track Your Results

Once you've spent time getting your content out into the world, you need to figure out if what you're doing is working. Making use of the free Google Analytics visitor tracker will help you do this.

By connecting your website up with this service, you will be able to get insights into where your visitors live, which pages on your site they landed on, which page they went to next and how long they spent browsing your site. All this is critical to know if you want any chance of plotting and planning your success. Once you know which your best sources of visitor referrals are and what people visiting your site are looking at the most, you can create further similar content and distribute it to the channels you know are proving fruitful.

To set up your website visitor tracking using Google Analytics, go here:

https://analytics.google.com/analytics/web

Under the Admin option, you should register a new account for your website. You'll then need to place the Google Analytics tracking code you're given onto your website. This is easiest done by installing the **Google Analytics** WordPress plugin, found in the plugin directory within your WordPress dashboard.

Now you're all set to start tracking visitors, page hits, visitors' countries and much more. Each time you put up a new blog post and announce it to the world, check your Google Analytics reports a couple of days later and you look for a new spike in traffic. Hit gold with a post that goes viral and you'll be able to see the effect of your hard work with an even bigger upturn in numbers.

Here's the main view from the Google Analytics dashboard on a new site that has shared three blog posts, shown by the spikes in visitor numbers on the graph. This view also shows the average time spent on your site and the countries that those visitors came from:

You can also get a view on which type of device your visitors are using to access your website from, whether that's mobile, tablet or desktop, as shown here:

Device Category	Acquisition			Behavior		
	Sessions ↓	% New Sessions	New Users	Bounce Rate	Pages / Session	
	980	90.71%	889	7.45%	2.80	
	% of Total: 100.00% (980)	Avg for View: 90.71% (0.00%)	% of Total: 100.00% (889)	Avg for View: 7.45% (0.00%)	Avg for View: 2.80 (0.00%)	
1. desktop	561 (57.24%)	92.69%	520 (58.49%)	8.91%	2.77	
2. mobile	326 (33.27%)	87.73%	286 (32.17%)	5.52%	2.65	
3. tablet	93 (9.49%)	89.25%	83 (9.34%)	5.38%	3.53	

The numbers coming from mobile or tablet may vary depending on your business type and implementation. For instance, if you're a fan of Instagram and you collect leads by sending people to your website from within the app, you will see a higher incidence of mobile traffic, as this is how people primarily access Instagram.

You can also enable demographics to be collected from visitors to your site so you can gain an insight into the hobbies and habits of those clicking on your pages, which may be of interest to you when researching your audience.

There's a wealth of information to explore so don't miss out. Pick a few of the more useful screens of data and use these to keep an eye on numbers and behaviours, then tailor your content and sharing habits accordingly.

You can download the Facebook Pixel Plugin and your printable Monthly Content Calendar at: http://crackingthewebsitecode.com/bonus

Chapter 9: Summary

- **Sharing doesn't have to be complicated.** Yes, it can be time consuming but you don't have to do it all manually. Use social sharing apps to schedule content and you'll free yourself up to do other more productive tasks.

- **Be consistent and persistent.** Once you've done the hard work and created some great content, get it out there being seen, often.

- **Share. A lot.** More sharing = more traffic to your site = more potential for sales.

- **Automate social sharing.** Use one or more of the many social sharing tools to get your content out to your audience regularly.

- **Play Google at its own game.** Two extra minutes adding good SEO markers could be the difference between you being never found on page 25 or being visible to all on page 1 of Google search.

- **Make a content creation plan.** And stick to it. If you don't keep on top of your goals, you're likely to go off track and get nowhere fast.

- **Use content scheduling tools.** Make the most of some of the free scheduling tools to get content ready in advance, giving you more time to do yoga or play golf. Or create even more content.

- **Track your results**. Use the free Google Analytics to keep tabs on visitor numbers, country of origin, popular pages and much more.

5 Ways To Convince People To Buy From You, Without Selling

"You can't convince anyone of anything.
You can only give them the right information,
so that they convince themselves"
~ Eben Pagan

You know you're worth investing in, right? I hope it's fair to say that you believe 100% in the products or services that you offer, so how do you convince your target audience member of the same?

Unless you're a natural born salesperson with an

unnerving desire to get in people's faces and shout about how great you are, it can feel like a daunting task to try to gain that confidence. But it can be much easier than you think. Let's look at five easy ways you can elevate yourself to trustworthy expert worth buying from, without running your mouth once.

1. Let Other People Sing Your Praises

There's nothing better than a recommendation from someone who has already enjoyed the experience of working with you or buying from you. Setting up a dedicated page of testimonies or adding one or two here and there on your website really speaks volumes. I mean, if other people are saying how great you are, you must have something going for you, right?

Testimonies can come from you asking for a few sentences on how your product or service helped someone and what they enjoyed the most about the experience, or they can be simple screenshots from social media or text messages. But wherever you source your recommendations from, make sure to ask the person you're quoting if it's ok to use their words before you slap them on your site and risk getting in trouble. Some people prefer to stay private and may not want the world to know they bought your product, so always ask first.

Showing a picture of the person alongside their quote can often increase trust more than just a quote alone, but test this out on your website and see if it makes any difference. Here's an example of one I'm using on my website that helps to sell this book for me, without me having to say a word:

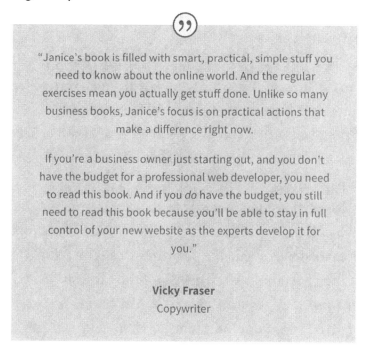

"Janice's book is filled with smart, practical, simple stuff you need to know about the online world. And the regular exercises mean you actually get stuff done. Unlike so many business books, Janice's focus is on practical actions that make a difference right now.

If you're a business owner just starting out, and you don't have the budget for a professional web developer, you need to read this book. And if you *do* have the budget, you still need to read this book because you'll be able to stay in full control of your new website as the experts develop it for you."

Vicky Fraser
Copywriter

2. Create An About Page That Sells

Most people who have a website tend to create an About page, because, well, everyone has one of those don't they? The page usually involves drivelling on about who you are, what you do, what qualifications you have and what hobbies you get up to in your spare time.

Wrong idea.

Why do you think people come to your About page? Is it to learn how many kittens you have or what fancy degree you earned? No. The real reason they visit is to check out if you're worth getting more deeply involved with. They've come to see what you can offer, whether you and your business are congruent with their values and needs. They're not there to learn your life story. Well, not to start with anyway.

So let's rethink how you can use your About page and let's focus it more on what you can do for your potential customer who has come to see if you're a good fit.

Instead of writing about yourself, start with what you can do for others—specifically for that one person reading your page at that moment. Treat this core page as a mini sales letter. If someone lands here, they're much closer to purchasing your products or services than you probably realise, so make strides towards that sale by telling them what they need to know. This is not the same as just telling them *what they want to hear* as a platitude—you need to get across, in a genuine manner, what you can give and why anyone should listen to you or buy from you.

As with any sales page, start with a good headline that will draw readers in and give them an immediate understanding of what you can do for them, for example:

> ### Hi, I'm Janice and I help entrepreneurs get online and in front of their ideal customers, fast.

You could also ask questions that your ideal customer can identify with, then tell them about your solution. You can go one better by including how they can avoid a pain point at the same time, for example:

Do you struggle knowing how to get
more sales from your website?
I solve that by showing you how to
get your content seen by more of
the right people, without paying for ads.

Once you've hooked your reader in with your headline and a couple of points they can identify with, only then is it time to spell out why you're qualified to provide what you're offering. Add a short paragraph or two on how you got to where you are now and make it relatable by empathising with your reader and showing that you understand the struggles that they're having right now.

Tell them how you came up with a solution to the issues you've just described, which leads you nicely to talking about your product or service.

As we've discussed previously, be sure to talk about the benefits of your solution, allowing the reader to imagine how their life would change for the better after using your product. If your solution is not something that improves lives in a dramatic or tangible way, this may not be applicable, but you can still talk about the benefits of what you offer.

After the solution presentation, add a call to action to either sign up for your mailing list (with opt-in bribe of course) and/or buy your solution. Either way, don't let them leave without giving you their email address—see the next chapter for why and how to do this.

Once you're done with your mini-sales pitch, which is really about them and not you, you can then either go into your back story in more detail, or (best) link to a separate page where they can read your full life story. But only include this option if it would be of value and help show someone why you are the right person to satisfy their needs today. This may not be applicable if your business is presented as a brand name, rather than you as the personality fronting your brand. In that case, you could include the story of the brand, how it came to fruition and the people behind it.

By sending your readers to a separate story page, it keeps your About page free from clutter and is probably more likely to result in a sign-up to your list. It also means that only those truly interested in you, rather than just what you can do for them, will find their way to the long-form story page.

After you implement a well-rounded About page that's not *just* about you, you'll stop turning people away who aren't sure if what you offer is what they need—after reading your *new* About page, they will hopefully be even more enthused at the prospect of working with you, because of the solutions you've shown you are able to provide.

3. Use Case Studies

The proof is in the pudding, as they say. And by pudding, I'm talking about evidence that your product provides the solution it's supposed to.

Case studies are actually pretty easy to document. Take a handful of your previous overjoyed clients and ask them if it'd be ok for you to use their results on your website. If you offer a link to their business in the case study, they'll likely take you straight up on your offer.

When talking about a client and their successes, describe the reason this person or business came to you in the first place so that readers can relate if they're in a similar situation, show the results they got with your product—graphs and charts are perfect to help understanding—and maybe include a couple of paragraphs from the person to explain the types of success your solution helped bring about. And that's it.

4. Demonstrate

Sharing your expert knowledge and helping people find solutions to their problems is a beautiful way to sell yourself, without selling at all. Simply demonstrating your abilities can raise your expert status through the roof, especially if you genuinely help people along the way. This can be done with blog posts, video tutorials, audio in the form of podcasts or mp3 downloads, eBooks, courses— the list goes on.

If you can demonstrate your solutions using video, you

might also like to turn your teachings into a course. There are some fantastic platforms you can use to sell or even give away courses from, such as **Udemy.com** or **Teachable.com**. These sites make it very easy to throw a course together in no time and allow new students to discover your lessons.

Sharing is caring, and caring enables relationship-building, which brings trust and authority. So start creating content that demonstrates your area of expertise and don't forget to share.

5. Email Marketing

Successful entrepreneurs around the world agree on one thing, and it's coined by the phrase, "The money is in the list".

If you have a business, what's the one thing that you need, to survive? Sales.

And how do you get sales? By convincing people to buy.

And how do you convince them to buy? By building trust and relationships over time. Oh, and having a great product of course.

But how do you build that trust?

Enter email marketing.

If there was just one tactic I would impress upon you out of this whole book, it would be to concentrate on building your email list, so that you have potential clients on tap at the push of a Send button, to market your products to.

In the next chapter I'll go into email marketing in more detail, but for now, just know that it's not an optional extra, it's not something you should implement when you *get time* (i.e. most probably never), it's imperative to start and grow your list today.

Chapter 10: Summary

- **Get other people to show off your talents** by using testimonials and social proof.

- **Get your About page in order** so that it sells you to those who come to learn more.

- **Gather case studies** and detail them on your website. Proof of how your product or service has worked for others is priceless.

- **Show your expert knowledge** about by providing demonstrative content that solves your ideal client's problems.

- **Build your list**. Just do it. Like now. Read the next chapter immediately to get the lowdown.

Secure Your Business' Future
By Building Your Email List

*"I have literally built a multi-million dollar
business on the strength of my email list. Ninety
percent of my income comes from it."*
~ Michael Hyatt

As we enter the final chapters of the book, we're onto the
parts you've probably been waiting for, where we finally
get into the nitty gritty of making some money, moolah,
cash, notes, spondoolies, whatever you want to call it. So
let's start by looking at what I consider to be the most

important and non-negotiable way of growing your business—building a list of potential clients.

List building and the follow up action of email marketing can make a mediocre business fly if done well, so it's important to firstly start doing it, and secondly, become good at it.

Each step of the process of building a list of potential clients and marketing to them is not complicated. And once you set up a couple of pages on your website, much of it will happen on autopilot.

Let's look at getting people onto your list.

Beware Social Media!

Think about this for a moment—you've probably heard of people having their Facebook pages shutdown, usually for violation of terms of service, almost always without warning and often irretrievably. If you're like many entrepreneurs, you will have hundreds or even thousands of people who are fans of your business pages, who you reach regularly with your content. So what happens when your account gets shutdown? You lose all connection to those people. You lose the ability to put your product in front of them. You can no longer contact those people, full stop. And that's where the problem lies.

You don't own your Facebook account, nor your Instagram or Twitter or any other social media account. This should spell danger to you. One false move or a backhanded report of misconduct by one of your competitors and you can be shutdown in an instant. It's act first, investigate later for the social media bosses. And this could leave you without a large part of your audience for quite some time, possibly forever.

What do you do then?

The answer lies in saving your social media contacts to your own personal database. And by database, I mean list of email addresses. So how do you get hold of those precious emails? By trading for something of value. Simple.

As an entrepreneur, you usually have something that your customers are interested in, whether that's solutions to their problems, products that fulfil their desires or a presence that fits in with their ideals. Potential new clients are often willing to trade you some of what you have for their email address. It's a fair deal, as long as you offer something that feels valuable to them.

This is where it becomes interesting. Determining what your audience see as valuable will define your success in this trading process. Offer the wrong thing and you won't tempt many to trade, but put something appealing up for grabs and you've got your deal.

If you didn't realise it before, you need to take action towards getting people off social media and onto your website, to make that trade as soon as possible. Being left with no contacts should not be a position you ever want to find yourself in.

Incentives

In order to know what to offer as your incentive to trade, you need to get into the mind of your potential clients again. Ask yourself what would really help them, then design something simple but valuable, based around this idea. Your incentive is often referred to as a lead magnet, because it's there to attract leads into your business.

Your lead magnet can be as simple as a 10 point checklist, or a cheatsheet for getting a task done—it doesn't have to be too extensive or complex. Popular options for lead magnets include short eBooks, email courses, webinars and coupon codes. Whatever you choose to offer, just be sure that it's relevant for your audience and the content sits well within your overall strategy. The trade will then deliver subscribers that are likely to be interested in your other products.

Creating Lead Magnets

If you're now racking your brain wondering how on earth you're going to create something good enough to give away on your site, don't worry, you don't need any design skills. That's right, none whatsoever. You can design your giveaway to look extremely professional, for free.

Do you know what one of the most popular programs for designing lead magnet content is? Microsoft Word. Yes, that simple word-processing program that almost everyone owns is responsible for a large percentage of all eBook downloads today. That's not to say that it gives you *ultimate* quality eBook designs, it doesn't. But if you don't have any graphic design software or simply aren't that artistic, you can most definitely design your giveaway in Word. Another option, if your eBook is in the style of a set of bullet points rather than an essay, is Microsoft Powerpoint. So don't think you need fancy software to write an eBook—you don't. Apple's Pages and Keynote programs are similar options you can use if you have a Mac.

If you're creating an eBook as your lead magnet and are using Word or Pages, here are my suggestions to make your content shine:

- **Use big, bold headings** for each chapter or section title in your eBook.
- **Choose different fonts** for the headings and the main body text and keep them consistent throughout.
- **Make sure your fonts are readable**. Test your content on a computer, tablet and mobile to be sure.
- **Put a solid, dark border** around the edge of all the pages, to draw the eye into the centre of the page and to your main content.
- **Don't go mad with colours** unless you know what you're doing. Hot pink might be your favourite

colour today, but think of those poor people trying to read your document and having hot pink borders etched indelibly onto their eyeballs! Calm, neutral tones work well, blues and greens are easy on the eyes, but it's good to add the occasional flash of colour to highlight points as needed.

- **Use images to enhance your words**, but only add them at appropriate places, where they compliment the text. Don't just add images for the sake of making it pretty, you'll detract from the text if you go overboard just to fill up space. Your readers are not daft, they will smell a filler a mile off.

Another way to create an impressive looking download is to use the online design tool at Canva.com. As I showed you in Chapter 7, Canva provides all sorts of layouts, many completely free to use—all you have to do is add your text, change the pictures or colours to suit yourself, and you've got a great looking design in no time.

Canva will even allow you to create multi-page documents, so if you're giving away more than a single sheet, you could actually create your whole eBook in this way. This might be great in theory but if you've got a lot of text to lay out, it might slow you down as there will be a lot of mouse clicking and layout trials involved.

If you have no desire to spend time creating your own cover for your eBook and just want it done for you, you might want to look for someone offering this service at

fiverr.com. Here, you can get a beautiful cover designed for $5 by someone who does this day in, day out. Search for 'eBook cover design' within fiverr and look for someone with impressive designs, a good rating and short waiting list.

If you're just starting out, my advice would be to create your download in Word or Pages then use Canva or fiverr to get a really nice cover for your eBook. Download the cover image, place it into the first page of your document and you've completed your eBook. Save it in PDF format and it's ready to use as your lead magnet on your website.

Hand It Over

So how does the trading of lead magnet for email address work? It's usually done on your website, by means of a landing page, sometimes also called a squeeze page. This is where you make the offer of a gift for your visitor and ask them to put in their email address to get it. It's a very simple concept and works a treat if you set out the right offer for your audience.

If you use a service such as Lead Pages, you can get a landing page together in about 5 minutes flat. The best thing about LeadPages is that they have proven templates that convert like crazy, all you have to do is pick one you like the look of, replace the words and images with your own and hook it up to your email autoresponder service.

If you don't want the added expense of using a service such as Lead Pages to create landing pages with, you can create your own on your website. When you do this, try to keep the page as free from distractions as possible, because the only thing you want to happen on that page is for a visitor to put in their email address. Get rid of the header, menu options, sidebar and footer, provided your website theme allows it. With only the offer staring them in the face, people viewing your page are far more likely to take action and sign up, as long as it's something that genuinely interests them.

If your WordPress theme doesn't support blank pages, you can use a plugin to create landing pages for free. There are a number available, just search for Landing Page in the add plugin area.

Pop-Ups — Annoying or Brilliant?

There are other ways to get people to sign up to your list from your website, even if they don't visit your lead magnet page. Here's one—pop-ups.

It can be tough to decide whether to use pop-ups on your website, to nudge your visitors into signing up to your list. From a visitor point of view, it can be somewhat annoying when you're faced with a pop-up and all you're trying to do is read the damn web page, I will agree with that. But site owners who do use pop-ups will generally enjoy a much higher sign-up rate than those who don't. So ask yourself, do you want more sign-ups or not?

If you're on the fence about using pop-ups on your site, I have just two words for you:

Do it, now.

Okay that was three words but it was worth the extra one to emphasise how strongly I feel about it.

From my own experience I can tell you that once I started using pop-ups to grab my website visitors' attention, my sign-up rate multiplied by over twelve times. You read that right, I get twelve times more sign ups using a pop-up offer than I do by using the same sign-up form sat quietly in the sidebar.

People have become a bit blasé about subscription forms in the sidebar of web pages. They're the new norm and are therefore often ignored. Getting all up in your visitors' faces with an offer they can't *not* read, even if they do sometimes close it down, is better than not being noticed at all.

Whether you set your pop-up to activate just a few seconds after someone lands on your page or right as they're about to hit the X to exit is neither here nor there. Try it both ways and see which get you the best results. But *do* try it—only *your* results will let you know if it's a smart decision for your business.

There are a number of great pop-up and opt-in form creation products, some of which you install on your site, others that are cloud-based and require no installation. Here are the ones that work with WordPress that I would recommend looking into, even though there are also many more on the market:

- **Pop-Up Domination** — works remotely so will not interfere with your website styling and won't slow it down. Allows every type of opt-in you can think of. A high quality and well-supported product.
- **Mail Munch** — provides several types of opt-in forms and is free to use if you don't mind the small MailMunch logo under your forms. Design your forms away from your website and copy the code provided.
- **Bloom** — a WordPress plugin that comes with the Elegant Themes full suite of themes and plugins. This one is great if you're also looking to purchase a new theme—this package comes with 87 of them, so take your pick.
- **Optin Monster** — similar to MailMunch, providing several options for opt-in forms and exit pop-ups. It includes split-testing and integration with many of the most popular email marketing providers. Use of Optin Monster incurs a monthly or annual fee.
- **Sumo Me** — online service that provides some unique opt-in formats, such as full-screen option placed above your web page, forcing visitors to either sign up or scroll down past it to continue. Free to use if you don't mind sumo-me branding on your forms.
- **Thrive Leads** — part of the Thrives Themes package—a complete suite of optins, landing pages,

website builder, headline optimiser and much more, for a reasonabe monthly fee. High quality and highly recommended.

If you're not using pop-ups on your site, try it, it won't hurt and it will almost certainly help your list grow, which potentially means more additions to your buyers list.

Email Marketing

Email marketing is undoubtedly *the* best way to capitalise on those leads that just came through your sales funnel via your lead magnet sign up, through your landing page or pop-up opt-in form.

When email marketing is done well, it can lead to long-term customers that can't wait to get their credit card out to buy your next product. So what is email marketing really about, and how can *you* be one of the success stories?

Ray Higdon, network marketing expert, said:

"Prospecting for new customers should indeed be done whenever the opportunity randomly arises, but marketing is something that should always done intentionally".

And that's what email marketing is—writing intentionally, with a purpose—that being to help people get to know you, respect you and ultimately want to work with or buy from you.

Realise The Potential

Don't mistake the people who signed up for your lead magnet as new customers—they're not, yet. Also don't think the hard work is done once you have that all-important email address—it's not. Getting someone onto your email list is just the beginning of a *hopefully* long and meaningful relationship.

You probably either love or hate the idea of email marketing. If you view owning that list of contacts purely as an opportunity to make money, then you will probably not do well with it. Why? Because it's not natural to one minute ask someone for their email address, and the next ask if they want to spend their hard-earned cash on a product they've not yet even heard of. You probably wouldn't do it face-to-face, so it's likely it'll feel strange doing it via email too. And if it feels strange or fake, then you're not being true to yourself.

If you think of email marketing as a way to further your relationship with the people kind enough to hand over their email address, you will not resent or fear it. And if you get your email marketing right, you may just come to love it, because it could turn out to be the most lucrative part of your business.

One of my internet marketing colleagues claims that every person added to his email list is worth $1000. If that's true and he had just 1000 people on his list, that's a million big bucks! I think it's safe to say he has *way* more than 1000 on his list, so you do the maths.

Let's get real though—even if you only have 1% of the success my internet marketing guru friend has, that could be $10 you earn for every person you add to your list. So even if it costs you $2 to add each person to your list using paid ads, it's worth sitting up and listening to isn't it?

What If They Don't Like Me?

It can be a scary prospect to email people who you don't really know, I mean what do you talk about? And what if they don't like your content and promptly unsubscribe? I have to tell you it's time to get over both of these silly fears, because they are silly. In order to get to the people who *are* a perfect fit for your business, you have to weed out those that aren't. And the only way to do this is to send out your emails, share your content in your unique, unfiltered way, and see who stays. *They* are the ones who are most likely to become your next customers and the ones you want to keep marketing to.

I Can't Write!

I know writing is not everyone's cup of tea and if you struggle to even send a text message, making up a whole series of emails is going to be quite daunting. But I do believe everyone can do this if it's approached simply.

Email marketing is not about creating a work of art. It's not about spelling every single word correctly or making sure you don't offend anyone, it's about showing your readers exactly who you are and polarising them one way or another. Those that don't like what you talk about or how you say it can go elsewhere because you probably wouldn't want to work with them anyway. Email marketing is about you being you and giving your readers a true taste of what you're all about. So if you can't spell, so what? If English is not your first language or you don't get every sentence grammatically perfect, so what? Just be yourself—that will be what wins over the people that matter.

What To Write About

When someone first signs up to your email list either in exchange for a lead magnet or as a newsletter subscriber, they're not likely to know much about you, your business, or how you can help them. So the first email to send after your lead magnet delivery email should be a welcome message, thanking them for signing up for your offer and telling them what they're likely to receive from you in future. You could also add a short background story about yourself or your business but keep it short and sweet.

What next? To create that trust and authority, you could then send out some of your best content, whether that's a summary of a few your most popular blog posts, another free resource or a short piece of content designed exclusively for your subscribers. Make it interesting, useful and related to the topic of your lead magnet, website content or business. No sales pitches yet please!

And then what? More of the same! Your next couple of emails should be built upon the same principles—offering help, ideas and valuable content, and letting your personality shine through. Your subscribers should start to feel like you "get" them and that you know what you're talking about.

Storytelling

The best way to show off your personality is to write how you speak. Can you hear my voice as you read this? That's because I'm using that very technique here. I want this book to be my way of reaching out to you and you getting to know me. I want it to be so easy to read that you feel like you can hear me speaking the words right to you, and to you alone. You might not know the exact slant of my British accent or how I like to pull emoticon faces as I end my sentences, but I hope you can "hear" me in your head.

After receiving a few getting-to-know-you emails, your readers will have started to form an impression of you. They will hopefully have got some value from your content and have warmed to you. Once your subscribers are in this state, you can start introducing your products or services. No one *loves* being intentionally sold to, so it's your job to find a way to providing great content, then to create a seamless link to something you have to offer.

As an example, if you're someone who helps bloggers create stunning content that people will want to share, you may have sent a few emails with some techniques that your readers may want to try out. One of those emails could be a story of how using beautiful images helped your blog post to be shared 5,843 times in a day. Leading on from that it would be a great opportunity to mention a course that you offer, where you show people *exactly* how you create this type of image and the techniques you used to get so many shares in one day. By having a story lead into the action of asking for the sale, you will feel less pushy and your content will flow more naturally from story to sale. This method of marketing should sit better with you if you're a bit shy when it comes to showing off your products or asking for money.

Repeat The Cycle

Asking someone to invest money in you or your business can feel uncomfortable, but it doesn't have to if you truly believe in your product and know that the person making that investment is going to get something useful out of it. It would actually be a travesty if you knew you could help people but you *didn't* pass on that knowledge. Good things are meant to be shared and you shouldn't feel bad doing that in exchange for money, if it's what your customer wants.

Email marketing can be done in cycles, so once the sale has been offered once or twice in consecutive emails, go back to the start and again send out more helpful content before working up to another offer. This cycle works to provide value, gain trust and authority, and ultimately get those who didn't buy last time one step closer to wanting your next set of premium content.

Once you've made the offer in your email, make sure not to ask your reader to do anything else apart from click through to buy your product. If you give them any more options, you risk taking the focus off the main action, which is getting that sale.

How Often Should You Email?

This question is often a hot topic of discussion amongst marketers—and don't forget *you* are a marketer if you have something to offer. There are two very different camps when it comes to email marketing.

Firstly, there are those who say that emailing every single day, or at least every week day, works best. And indeed, many people making a killing online use this tactic. The theory behind this is that your list members will come to *expect* to hear from you every day, so when your email shows up offering a product for sale now and again, it will feel like just another of your emails and therefore be more likely to be accepted as part of the normal routine.

Another reason for emailing every day is to build up trust with your reader much quicker. If you can put half an hour aside every day to write an email that entertains, adds value or helps your reader out in some way, I say go for it, because the people who do this are adamant it gets them better conversion rates when it comes to sales.

The only thing you *may* notice if you email every day is that you get a faster drop-off rate—people unsubscribing. But if you think of this as quickly weeding out those who really aren't interested in what you have to offer, it's not such a bad thing. After all, why have people on your list who are never going to buy from you? You're not charity so think of it as a good business move.

The other side of the fence would have you only email once a week or once a fortnight, or just when you have something worth sending out. This routine works for some as it means you don't feel overwhelmed with having to come up with new content as often. With the extra time between emails, you can spend time crafting a fuller message with possibly more in-depth content.

The only slight issue with this is that people are in a hurry and can be overwhelmed by long emails, so you risk your hard work going to waste. A good way to capitalise on your content is to also create a blog post from it—repurposing content like this gives you multiple ways to be found. Make it evergreen content and it will never become irrelevant either.

By emailing less often, it will take your readers longer to get to know you, but if you can be patient and not be tempted to ask for the sale too soon, this could work for you.

I would advocate being regular with your emails on whichever schedule you choose—consistency brings respect and is more likely to gain your readers' trust.

There are some, in fact *many*, marketers who ask you to buy something in every single email, but these are more often than not in the internet marketing niche, where new tools are launching daily and where there is serious money to be made out of someone clicking your link to buy. I don't particularly like this kind of incessant selling and often unsubscribe very quickly from these type of lists. The point is, how you view other people's email techniques should give you a hint as to how you want to run your own email campaigns, so pick what feels right to you and make sure to stick to a regular schedule, then adjust if you don't get the results you hoped.

One technique that I would recommend you use in every email, no matter how often that occurs, is this— always add a call to action. The quicker your reader gets used to you asking them to perform an action, the easier it will be for you to eventually ask them to buy your product. If you hardly ever ask for an action to be taken, that plea for a sale may come across more sales-like and not sit as easy with your readers. You can ask them to do anything from clicking a link to read the full blog post, to filling in a quick survey, to replying to your email with their biggest struggles so that you can help solve them. Make sure to ask for an action in every email, so that it becomes normal to ask and normal for your reader to oblige.

Automate The Process

I hope you realise that whenever you sign up for someone else's lead magnet, they're not actually sat at the computer typing a thank-you email to you. You must know that the delivery of your lead magnet and the emails that come with it are automated, right?

Ok, so how do you implement that kind of cleverness in your own business? By signing up to an email autoresponder service.

As the name suggests, an autoresponder responds automatically with an email or series of emails, usually when triggered by an event. So when someone fills in your opt-in form, your autoresponder receives their details and is prompted to start sending out messages at the times and days you specify.

As you can imagine, this can save a lot of time and can enable you to deliver emails to new subscribers even when you're in bed. Brilliant.

So that list of emails we outlined above can all be pre-programmed into your autoresponder sequence and sent out the required number of days after sign up.

There are a number of popular autoresponder tools available on the market, some of which are free to use when you have a lower number of subscribers, so it's a no brainer to get started. Most have a free trial period for you to see how you get along with their services and user interface.

One of most popular free autoresponders is **MailChimp**. It's cost-free to send regular newsletters to up to 2000 subscribers, so this gives you plenty of time to start building your list, practicing your email marketing techniques and start making sales. If you want to use the autoresponder features and send out a series of pre-written automated messages, there's a small fee each month but it's totally worth it.

Two other popular autoresponders at the lower end of the cost scale are **GetResponse** and **Aweber**. These, as well as MailChimp, are usually the most easily integrated with the popular opt-in services, so I would recommend starting with one of these.

Once you start making sales from your list and feel the need to segment your list into different streams, it may be time to upgrade to one of the more advanced autoresponder services, such as Ontraport or Infusionsoft. But get regular updates going out first before you go getting too advanced.

Chapter 11: Summary

- **List building** should be considered a mandatory part of building your online business. Without leads coming in on a regular basis, you don't have many ways to market directly to people who are interested in what you have to offer.

- **Creating a lead magnet** is the easiest way to initiate the trade of email address for useful content so this should be put into place if you don't currently have one.

- **Use pop-up opt-in forms** to gather targeted subscribers using your lead magnet as a trade. The more people on your list, the better your sales figures have potential to be.

- **Regular email marketing** is the intentional act of turning those people who *may* be interested in your products or services into loyal customers. Keep your longer term goal in mind each time you use email marketing to get in touch with your subscribers and remember to deliver value as often as possible.

- **Write how you speak**. The quickest way to get to know someone, without being face-to-face, is by writing in your spoken voice. Use the same language you would use in real life, rant if you normally like to rant, swear if you need to! Just be yourself and your personality will fly off the page, helping the readers who are destined to stay on your list keep receiving, and those who don't suit your ideals to get off your list completely.

- **Be regular and intentional.** Create your content and send it out on a regular schedule, whether that's daily, weekly or even monthly. Keep in mind why you are sending out each email and make it count.

- **Automate lead magnet delivery** and the first few emails in your sequence by using an autoresponder service. It will save you time and you can make money while you sleep. Epic.

If You Can't Be Good,
Be Careful

"Intelligent or not, we all make mistakes and perhaps the intelligent mistakes are the worst, because so much careful thought has gone into them."
~ Peter Ustinov

My friend Joe lost his website completely recently. Imagine the terror in his mind when he realised everything he'd worked so hard to create was simply gone.

Normally this wouldn't be an issue as you'd be able to

reinstall the site from a backup. But Joe didn't know about backups. Or security for that matter either. So his loss was pretty catastrophic.

Although protection against loss or attack is not in the least bit sexy, it is a must, and if you haven't got it in hand, I suggest you get it sorted right away.

WordPress offers a certain level of security, but that alone is not enough. Any time you install a new plugin or upgrade to a new version of WordPress, you could find that your site is no longer functioning as it should, or that you can't log in at all. As well as being an embarrassment for your business, this can be a real pain to resolve, the worst case being that you lose your site completely and have to start over. I don't mean to scare you—that hardly ever happens really—but you don't want to be the unlucky and unprotected one.

The other ridiculously easy way to lose your website is by leaving it open to attack. Don't be fooled into thinking a hacker is one guy (or girl), sat in his bedroom, tapping away at the keyboard until he figures out your password— it's not. Most hack attempts are performed by automated software called bots, that go scouring the internet for vulnerabilities. They'll use backdoor methods to force their way in and if you're not protected, down goes your site.

Once inside, hackers can plant dubious code and run scripts to send thousands of spam emails, increasing their presence on the internet and possibly crashing your server in the process. If your website goes down, you may have to spend a small fortune to get a specialist to clean up the mess and *hopefully* recover it for you.

I'm assuming this doesn't sound like fun to you, so what can you do to protect yourself against these risks? The good news is, in just a few easy steps, you can protect your site from much of the nonsense that goes on in those shady corners of the internet.

None of the solutions are difficult or time-consuming to implement, and you can set and forget in most cases.

Login Security

When you first set up WordPress, you may end up with the default username of *admin*. Huh, great choice WordPress—this is the first username any hacker will try when attempting to force his way into your site. The sophisticated software hackers use to break in to your site can test out hundreds of passwords on your site within seconds, and it's all automated.

The best way to stop these so-called brute force attacks, is to create a new administrator account with a completely different name than the default—something that can't be easily guessed. Once you have a new administrator account in place, you should login using those new user credentials and then delete the original admin user.

You—one, hackers—zero.

But don't think you're finished with problems with logins yet. If a hacker is dead set on getting into your site, they will run software to try to login over and over, which could also potentially take your website down. An easy way around this is to limit the number of login attempts any one computer can make before being blocked. As you probably guessed, there's a WordPress plugin to handle that, with the obvious name, **Limit Login Attempts**. Install it and set the number of failed logins you're prepared to allow.

Winning.

I hope I don't need to mention the fact that you should always use secure passwords, not only for your website login but everywhere online. The most secure are those that don't resemble real words, have a combination of numbers, letters, uppercase, lowercase and special characters in them, and are longer than 8 characters. When you choose a password for your site, you may be shown a sliding scale of how secure yours is. Get it to the highest level you can for maximum protection.

Backups

For a free backup solution, I'd recommend a WordPress plugin called **BackWPup**. This is very easy to set up and will automatically take backups of your whole site—files and database—on a regular basis. If your website content is changing daily, I'd recommend a daily backup, or less frequently if you're more of an occasional blogger.

Backups from BackWPup can be stored in various

locations, including Dropbox, Google Drive or on your website's server. I wouldn't recommend using the latter because if your site's server goes down, you won't be able to retrieve that backup file to restore your site with. I tend to use Dropbox for my backups, as it's a place that's always accessible and once the backup schedule is set, I can forget about it. If anything goes wrong with the backup process, you'll receive an email letting you know. If this happens, you can go in and try a manual backup to figure out if there's a problem or if it was a temporary glitch.

Another couple of plugins you can use to take a backup of a complete website, or transfer it to another host or domain are **Duplicator** and **WPClone**. Both work extremely well and are good as manual backup options, should your main backup solution fail.

Security

You will find numerous website security solutions on the market. One of the more reputable and commonly used free plugins is **Wordfence**, which, according to its website blurb, "continuously prevents, patrols and protects your WordPress websites against today's ultra-advanced cyber attacks, hacks and online security threats". It will also check your plugins are up-to-date and send you an email with the details of any required updates. Overall, this is a great solution, for free.

Another excellent plugin is **iThemes Security**, which guides you through securing your site and has a Pro upgrade available if you want the ultimate features.

Whichever solution you employ, don't forget that each tool is only as good as its last successful security block, so read reviews and go with the one that offers the best solution for your website's needs, but always take backups to guard yourself from loss too.

Updates

Believe it or not, even the WordPress software itself poses a risk to your website. If not kept up-to-date with the latest security patches, your website is at risk—even with a security solution in place.

Vulnerabilities in themes and plugins can also pose a threat, so it's best to go into your admin area and update both of these regularly—once a week or fortnight should be enough.

Chapter 12: Summary

- **Secure your WordPress login.** Create a new admin username that no one can guess and remove the original admin user.

- **Keep passwords secure**. Use strong passwords, containing letters, numbers and special characters and keep them nice and long.

- **Backups and security are not optional**. Unless you want to risk losing your website. Deploy both and set to work on autopilot.

- **Update WordPress and plugins regularly**. Often, these are the places security loopholes are found, so stay safe and stay up to date. Don't forget to backup first, just in case.

6 Opportunities To Make Money From Your Website

"If you make customers unhappy in the physical world, they might each tell 6 friends. If you make customers unhappy on the Internet, they can each tell 6,000 friends."
~ Unknown

There's no doubt that you can make money from your website, people are doing it all over the world right now. But if you're just setting up your site or you haven't yet successfully monetised yours, you may like some ideas to get you started. Let's have a look at six simple ways to make money from your website, some of which can be implemented within a few minutes and with very little effort.

1. Sell Your Own Creations

Creating your own products sounds like a lot of effort, and it can be. But think about this—the highest profits are most often made by selling your own creations, especially digital downloads such as eBooks, software or music. Why? Because you create them once, sell multiple times and all the profits are all yours. That's why it's such an attractive way to monetise your website. And that's also why this first option will be the most expansive.

If you're an entrepreneur, the chances are that you're an expert in a specific field and you know information that many others don't. This gives you the perfect opportunity to capitalise. If your area of expertise is knowledge- or experience-based, creating products in the form of digital downloads could be something that comes very easily to you. And if you *are* an expert, it's highly likely that what you know will roll of your tongue and onto the page quite readily, making the process of creating your products super quick.

When I started writing this book, one of my main motivations was to help people like you get better results with your website by sharing what I know. I actually took a publishing course so that I could make this book the very best it could be, but in this digital age there's no need to go that far, in fact it's more than acceptable to create downloadable PDFs that are less tightly regimented than a physical book. They still need to read well and be engaging, but this opens the way for absolutely anyone to sell digital products. A Word document with basic formatting and an attractive cover, saved as a PDF, sold from a single sales page can do very well, as long as it fulfils the promises you claim you'll deliver.

If you want to start selling digital downloads on your website, there are a number of WordPress plugins that will help you do that very easily. One of the most highly regarded is **Easy Digital Downloads**, which is free to use and offers all the basic shopping cart and payment functionality to get you started. However, as with most eCommerce solutions, useful add-ons such as automatic integration with your autoresponder software come at a premium. But if your store generates any more than a handful of orders every month, the fees for these extensions shouldn't be an obstacle.

Making profits selling your own creations doesn't have to stop with digital downloads—physical products are also popular to sell online. Take a hand-made children's clothing business for example—there's a certain type of person that will seek out this range of items online, and if you can tap into who exactly those people are, you could have the perfect customers for your items, without you having to split the profits with a middle man.

Two of the other most popular services for selling goods online are **WooCommerce** and **Shopify**. They each have their own merits but both make the process of selling goods online fairly pain-free, which is great news for creative types who don't care to get too technical.

The WooCommerce solution can be integrated into your own website using its free WordPress plugin, which enables you to have products on sale very quickly by simply providing an image, description and price. Paypal Standard integration is included for free, and within a few minutes you can be setup and ready to sell. If you're already familiar with the WordPress user interface, adding WooCommerce should be fairly straight forward for you.

Shopify is a slightly different solution as it is hosted on Shopify's own platform rather than on your website's server. This can make for a speedier shopping experience from a customer's point of view, especially if you have hundreds of products for sale. Shopify is purported to be one of the easiest ways to sell online but it does come at a price. Currently, their basic online store package costs $29 per month, but if it's an easy solution you are looking for then this may suit you.

Both WooCommerce and Shopify provide themes you can apply to your store, to give them a more unique look. Both provide a few free themes but also offer some attractive paid options. These are entirely optional.

Whichever solution you decide upon, keep in mind

that selling your own creations will net you a very healthy profit and should always be considered before other forms of monetisation. Having your own products, especially information-based digital downloads, will also help position you as the go-to expert in your field, which will in turn allow you to command a larger fee.

2. Use Affiliate Offers

If you don't yet have anything of your own to offer or are still in the process of creating something, why not use affiliate offers to get started? Affiliate schemes allow you to make a commission every time a sale results from you recommending someone else's product. Many companies offer affiliate commissions so always check for any such opportunities in the main menu area or the footer of websites that sell products in your niche.

Affiliate programs often supply banner graphics you can use on your website, so all you have to do is paste a simple piece of code into an area on your sidebar or into a blog post, and you're all set to start referring and earning.

Popular places to find affiliate offers in the information or software niche are clickbank.com and jvzoo.com, but if you type into Google search *"your-niche affiliate"*, replacing *your-niche* with your area of interest, you will usually find other referral programs to look in to.

Some social networks—Facebook in particular—don't allow links to known affiliate products, especially in the make money online, dating and adult-only markets, so if you attempt to link directly to an offer in one of these niches, your post will most likely be rejected. Even worse, if you are a repeat offender, you risk having your account suspended or even banned, so you will need to find a way around this.

One method—the one I'd recommend, whether you're promoting something that Facebook considers inappropriate or not—is to have the clickable link go to a landing page, where visitors must then put in their email address to get to the affiliate offer page. Putting a landing page between Facebook and the offer page means you don't have to worry about landing in Facebook jail. Not for that reason anyway. Facebook has lots of other reasons to make you do time. Using an intermediate landing page also means you have a set of email addresses to follow up with later.

Another method of getting around using banned URLs is to use what's known as link cloaking software. You tell the software your URL and it gives you back a new URL to use, having disguised the real destination behind your original link. This enables you to send visitors straight to the offer page, should you choose to do this.

The link cloaking method would be my second choice, for two reasons. First, if you send traffic straight to the offer page, you won't add any email addresses to your list. This means you can't follow up with those who clicked the link, to provide more information and hopefully convert them into buyers. Secondly, if your link goes straight to the offer page, you're unlikely to be able to track visitor numbers or use Facebook retargeting pixel to advertise to the same people again. As affiliate pages are not usually ones you have administrator's access to, you won't be able to add your retargeting pixel or use Google Analytics to dive into your statistics. Either way, delivering visitors straight to an offer will usually be a much more expensive way of getting leads or sales, because everyone clicking your link disappears into what's effectively an internet black hole. My advice would be to set up a landing page and only marshall those who are truly interested onto your list, to follow up with and sell to later. You may want to use a lead magnet to exchange for an email address for an even more effective and targeted capture method.

Make sure to also install the Facebook pixel on your landing page, so you can place a highly targeted Facebook ad later, set to appear only to those people who clicked your link previously.

3. Teach What You Know

Are you a specialist in something? Do you know more than other people know about a certain topic? If so, why not teach what you know? Running online courses is a great way to share your knowledge and set you up as an expert in your field.

For example, if you're a furniture restoration expert, could you create a series of short videos showing easy techniques to give a new finish to old furniture, that anyone can try at home. By doing so, this shows off your skills and expertise, builds you up as an authority and gives you visibility in the community. Then, when someone has a restoration job that is not as simple as a quick treatment they can do themselves, who do you think they'll call first? And that's how you become known, respected and trusted.

Creating courses is easier than you might think. Your course could be as simple as a set of emails that are drip-fed to people who subscribe to your eCourse. The email series could also contain links to videos prepared in advance, such as those as described above.

Getting a little more advanced but certainly not too complicated to manage, you could create a video course that allows people to learn at their own pace. Even if you don't want to go to the hassle of setting up a course on your own website, you can use services such as those at **Udemy.com** or **Teachable.com** to host your courses for you. All you have to do is create your lesson videos, upload them to the teaching platform then grab your course URL, ready to share.

With Udemy and Teachable, you keep a high percentage of the course fees, with the service provider taking a smaller cut. Alternatively, hosting courses on your own website may involve more setup fees and definitely more time, but then all the profits are yours to keep. I'd say if you have a large email list and think you can sell a high volume of courses, look into hosting them yourself for maximum profits. However, if your list is small, it's worth putting your course onto Udemy, as they will market it for you, bringing you many more sign-ups than you could probably achieve yourself.

Creating training videos doesn't require fancy production techniques. One option is to use Microsoft's Powerpoint or Apple's Keynote to create a slideshow, then record it while you do a voiceover using screen-recording software such as Camtasia. You don't have to appear in a single video if you don't want to. If you're anything like me, you can probably stand to talk over some slides, even if you never want to see your face on the big screen. Believe it or not, *most* courses don't feature the author talking to camera, so there's no need to panic or feel you're doing a lesser job than those who are confident to be visible.

Could you create a course about something you're passionate about? Does your business offer services that could be introduced with a short email or video course? Providing a lengthened sequence of emails or set of videos is a great way to build trust and show your expertise, which will mean more respect and more sales for you in future, so it's worth doing.

I believe everybody is an expert in something, even if you don't yet have the confidence or realisation to believe it. If you can talk about a subject and it brings you alive by doing so, there's a course inside you, I'm sure of it.

4. Invite Google To Advertise In Your Space

This may not be everyone's cup of tea, but if you have a space in your blog's header or sidebar that you don't mind giving up, your could potentially make a few extra notes by installing a Google AdSense or other similar advertising banner.

You're probably used to seeing this type of advert on other websites because they're such a popular way to make extra cash. The idea is that Google will show adverts to your visitors, based on their previous web browsing history. By doing this, the offers are likely to be highly relevant and therefore more click-worthy.

Many business owners would quite rightly shy away from this type of advertising because not only does it detract from the overall look and feel of your website, but it also encourages your visitors to click through to someone else's page. For these reasons, I wouldn't recommend installing one of these advertising banners unless you have considered the pros and cons fro your particular business.

But, if you do want to go ahead, and if you have anywhere upwards of a few hundred visitors a day to your site, you may benefit from Google AdSense earnings. You'll get the best returns if you place the banner above the fold—that is, visible before scrolling.

To get started with Google AdSense, go here:

http://google.com/adsense

5. Sell Advertising Space

By selling space on your blog for other people's advertisements, you could earn a tidy sum on the side. However, you will only attract advertisers to pay you to use space on your blog if you can prove your website is getting a certain volume of traffic first. With that said, offering advertising space may not be for those just setting up a website but it could be worth considering if you're well-established and attracting a higher number of visitors each month.

Once again though, as with the Google AdSense banner advertising, you must ask yourself if your website is sacred to you or if you are willing to compromise on its sleekness and consistency in favour of a bit of extra cash. It may alienate your visitors more than it makes you money.

Not having ventured into this form of advertising myself, I can't give advice on the best places to attract advertisers, but I believe web owners usually set up some sort of media kit to show off their audience statistics and marketability. It'd probably be helpful to contact influencers in your niche with a short email to introduce yourself and direct them to the opportunities on your site. The more traffic you can get to your site, the higher the fees you will be able to command.

6. Review And Recommend Products

Contacting companies directly is one way to obtain products to review and you may find they will send you items free of charge in return for a full review on your site, but again this may depend on your level of influence.

If you often mention products in your regular blog posts, such as if you're a food blogger and you talk about the best kitchen gadgets or specialist ingredients, you could monetise your blog with affiliate links for those products. Amazon Affiliates is one such program. By simply sharing a coded hyperlink that takes your reader straight to the product on Amazon, you could start earning commissions from one of the world's most popular online stores. The commissions from Amazon aren't huge, ranging from around 1 to 10%, but if you have a specialist blog where readers respect your word and your recommendations, you could do well. There are WordPress plugins available that enable you to show Amazon products on your site, complete with full product description, pictures and familiar Add To Cart or Buy Now buttons. This means your visitor has all the information to hand, to help make the buying decision right from within your website.

Similar to the Amazon affiliate program is the one from Prosperent.com. Here, you can also grab affiliate links to share on your website, earning a commission every time someone buys through your link. Prosperent makes every image "shoppable", making it a very attractive way to add affiliate links to your site. Prosperent is great for sharing a look, which could be a winning idea for blogs sharing lifestyle or fashion reports.

Chapter 13: Summary

- **Sell your own products**. If you don't yet have any, start creating today! The biggest margins can be made by selling your own creations.
- **Sell other people's products**. Why not? Good money can be made in commissions by recommending items useful to your audience.
- **Teach what you know**. Teaching increases your authority and positions you as an expert in your field, enabling you to charge more too.
- **Sell advertising**. If you have enough traction, invite others to pay you to be featured on your site.
- **Allow Google a little real estate**. Install Google AdSense and earn when people click. Simple idea but it won't make you a fortune unless you have high volumes of traffic to your site.
- **Review & recommend**. If you blog and could review products that others may be interested in hearing about, be sure to get an affiliate link and get paid for doing so.

What Next?

Now that you've read and hopefully digested the many aspects of running a successful website, it's time to step up to the plate and go from theory into full-on action.

You might feel like there's a lot to take in right now, and there is, I get it. But if you tackle each chapter and each concept one at a time, you'll at least start making progress *towards* your goals, not away from them, which is what doing nothing does. Slow and steady wins the race, okay?

I'd love nothing more than to hear from you, letting me know how you've started making improvements to your website, and more importantly, that you're seeing better results from it. Whether it's sales, subscribers or page views that you measure your success by, I want you to enjoy that higher level of satisfaction you came to this book with the hope of achieving.

I know I said it in the introduction, but I'll say it again —nothing will change without you putting some hard work in. So make sure you implement something new every week and you'll soon be on your way to realising your website's true potential. I have faith in you, just as you should in yourself.

Go and get cracking!

Free Gift Reminder

Cracking The Website Code comes with free bonus materials, to help you grow your business quicker and create the best website possible, so download yours today from:

http://crackingthewebsitecode.com/bonus

A Review, Please?

Did you enjoy *Cracking The Website Code*? If so, will you please **leave a review on Amazon** for me?

It would be lovely to hear how the book helped you, which parts you liked the most and what you are taking away to implement into your business right away.

As an independant author it's tough getting seen, but reviews do help make my book more visible to others, so I'd appreciate your support.

Thank you!

Janice

P.S. If you have spotted an error in my book that you'd like me to know about, please email me at janice@crackingthewebsitecode.com—I always like to hear if anything can be improved and I always reply personally.

About The Author

I've spent most of my adult life with my fingers stuck to a computer keyboard, knee deep in code. Websites have a strange attraction, I can't help but admit it. I've been called weird and that's fine by me, I understand that technology is not everyone's cup of tea. But I'm also not your typical girly-girl.

I grew up an only child so it might have taken me longer to learn to share my toys with others and to gain the social skills to not feel out of place in big groups. To compensate, I now tend to over-share—sorry if you're on the receiving end. Unless it's my chocolate—then you can think yourself lucky if you ever get a piece, and if you do, I'm probably watching you eating it, wishing it was still in my grubby hands instead. But I'm working on that.

I live in Preston with my husband, Steve, and our seven cats. Most of the bunch are beautiful British Shorthairs, the eldest two are rescue moggies. After sitting patiently at the RSPCA for seven months, we couldn't resist Mya and Gracie's lost little faces and have—we think—performed a minor miracle in bringing them back from unsociable and unloved to sweet, balanced creatures. The cats are all Princesses with a capital "P", the lot of them. Except Dexter, our only boy, who is a big soft sausage.

When I'm not playing crazy cat lady, I can often be found with my head in a book on a nutrition or food-for-health related topic. It fascinates me that so many diseases can be prevented or reversed by eating well. I try to spread the word and encourage others to take care with what they stuff into their cake-holes but the lure of the sugar- and fat-laden supermarket treats are too great for most, even for me unfortunately. I admit I'm not perfect although I do try to put quality nutrition into my body daily. In 2012 I even trained as a nutritionist and wrote a clean eating cookbook, which was also what sparked my addiction to the creative process of making eBooks.

Having been a professional portrait photographer for a couple of years in my twenties, I still love use my skills to take pictures of people, products or the ever-changing scenery. Scotland is one of our favourite places to visit to capture the beauty of the rugged and often untouched landscapes. It's fun to drive around the beautiful countryside, stalking deer, mimicking their deep, burp-like calls until we get close, then to snap hundreds of pictures of the bunch before they get wind of us. The males are magnificent up close, I can recommend a trip to The Highlands to see them in their natural habitat if you ever get the opportunity.

Random facts—I've always wanted a tattoo and to sing in a karaoke bar. I hate lifts and crowd crushes—yikes—get me out of there! I have an addiction to Indian food, reality TV and podcasts. My all-time musical love and influence is Prince—I've been crazy about him since I was about 12. He passed away just as I was getting ready to publish this book, hence the dedication at the front.

My other focus lately has been my family. With my mum's health declining, I've turned part-time carer, helping my dad out where I can, to take the pressure off him a little. I didn't think I'd be a natural carer but I don't feel quite as uncomfortable doing it as I feared—yet another example of being thrust into a situation and just having to get on with it. It's often not as bad as you imagined.

Which is why you should just dive in with whatever scares you the most, and do it like you mean business.

CPSIA information can be obtained at www.ICGtesting.com
Printed in the USA
LVOW11s1526260716

497830LV00007B/505/P